how to be a
better....

time
manager

how to be a better....

time
manager

Jane Smith

YOURS TO HAVE AND TO HOLD
BUT NOT TO COPY

First published in 1997
Reprinted 1998

Kogan Page Limited
120 Pentonville Road
London N1 9JN

British Library Cataloguing in Publication Data
A CIP record for this book is available from the British Library.
ISBN 0 7494 2375 7

Typeset by Intype London Ltd
Printed in England by Clays Ltd, St Ives plc

THE INDUSTRIAL SOCIETY

The Industrial Society stands for changing people's lives. In nearly eighty years of business, the Society has a unique record of transforming organisations by unlocking the potential of their people, bringing unswerving commitment to best practice and tempered by a mission to listen and learn from experience.

The Industrial Society's clear vision of ethics, excellence and learning at work has never been more important. Over 10,000 organisations, including most of the companies that are household names, benefit from corporate Society membership.

The Society works with these and non-member organisations, in a variety of ways – consultancy, management and skills training, in-house and public courses, information services and multi-media publishing. All this with the single vision – to unlock the potential of people and organisations by promoting ethical standards, excellence and learning at work.

If you would like to know more about The Industrial Society please contact us.

The Industrial Society
48 Bryanston Square
London
W1H 7LN
Telephone 0171 262 2401

The Industrial Society is a Registered Charity No. 290003

CONTENTS

HOW TO BE A BETTER...SERIES

Whether you are in a management position or aspiring to one, you are no doubt aware of the increasing need for self-improvement across a wide range of skills.

In recognition of this and sharing their commitment to management development at all levels, Kogan Page and The Industrial Society have joined forces to publish the How to be a Better . . . series.

Designed specifically with your needs in mind, the series covers all the core skills you need to make your mark as a high-performing and effective manager.

Enhanced by mini case studies and step-by-step guidance, the books in the series are written by acknowledged experts who impart their advice in a practical way which encourages effective action.

Now you can bring your management skills up to scratch *and* give your career prospects a boost with the How to be a Better . . . series!

Titles available are:
How to be Better at Giving Presentations
How to be a Better Problem Solver
How to be a Better Interviewer
How to be a Better Teambuilder
How to be a Better at Motivating People
How to be a Better Decision Maker
How to be a Better Communicator
How to be a Better Negotiator
How to be a Better Project Manager
How to Hold Better Meetings
How to be Better at Creativity
How to be Better at Writing Reports and Proposals
How to be a Better Time Manager

Forthcoming titles are:
How to be a Better Leader
How to be Better at Managing Change

Available from all good booksellers. For further information on the series, please contact:

Kogan Page, 120 Pentonville Road, London N1 9JN
Tel: 0171 278 0433   Fax: 0171 837 6348

INTRODUCTION

In this turbulent world we never seem to have enough time, yet there has never been so much time available to us. We live longer, we use less time to make and do things as we get more efficient and should therefore have more time to spare. Yet we have made this strange commodity into a competitive weapon, paying over the odds for speed. If we were wise, would we not take the price tag off time, and give ourselves time to stand and stare?

Charles Handy (1994) *The Empty Raincoat*, Arrow Business Books UK.

One of the consequences of poor time management for many people is that it tips their lives out of balance so that they don't pay enough attention to the things that are really important to them. All too often, work seems to take over a disproportionate part of our lives, with the result that we don't see our friends as often as we would like, our family life suffers and we have little time for relaxation and physical exercise.

But the paradox is that when work dominates the horizon to such an overwhelming extent, we are probably being neither as efficient nor as effective at work as we could be with a better organized lifestyle.

If you often work late or take work home, if you never stop for a lunch break, if you constantly feel that you have too much to do or that you are always rushing to meet deadlines, you should take a break now to look at the way you are organizing your work. It is just not possible to work ten hours a day, six days a week and still be effective. We all have limits on the amount of time within which can we we can do a good job; it's more important to use the that time well than to try to work more hours.

This book aims to help you identify where your time goes at the moment, what the problems are and how to plan to use your time better – both in the long and the shorter term. It also suggests lots of techniques that are commonly used for managing time: avoiding crisis management, making meetings more effective, delegating to other people, reducing interruptions and many more.

When you begin to put some of these techniques and approaches into practice, you will notice many changes in other parts of your life. For example, as you start to feel more relaxed and more in control of your time, it is likely that your health will improve and your confidence will grow. You will be able to give yourself more time for yourself – time to think, to relax, to take exercise, to learn and ultimately to develop your true potential.

1

THE PARADOX OF TIME

'I'd like to be able to manage my time better but I never seem to find the time' – this commonly heard light-hearted comment points to a common problem for most of us: how to find the time to achieve everything we would like in our lives. It is a particular problem at work because the time we spend there is formally defined. Poor time management leaves us feeling frustrated at the end of the working day. Tasks are not completed and we have to carry them forward, or even worse, we have to work late to get things done. And struggling to keep up standards when we are already tired only produces stress and poor quality work.

Although it is true that some people are short of time because they simply have too much to do, most of us would benefit from thinking about what we are doing with our time at the moment and how we would like to change this. Time is a valuable resource because it is non-renewable; to be an effective manager you need to learn how to manage your time well.

WHY DO WE NEED TO MANAGE OUR TIME BETTER?

Executive Stress, a survey by Allied Dunbar (January 1996), claims that most of the three million people who work in full-time professional and managerial jobs in Britain suffer from stress, nearly a quarter of them are under pressure from dead-lines and a further tenth from long hours and heavy workloads.

The experience of those who have learned to manage their time better tells us that astonishing improvements can be made by learning and using just one or two simple techniques.

Andy, a quality control manager in a pharmaceutical company, found continuous interruptions from his own staff a problem. Sometimes there was a genuine crisis, but more often, the problem could have been dealt with at a more mutually convenient time. In the end he made it known that anyone was welcome between 4.30 and 5.30 every day for a coffee and a chat. At the same time he made it clear that when his door was closed, he was not to be disturbed unless it was something really urgent. Now he has got the system going he finds that there has been a considerable reduction in the number of unnecessary interruptions.

Liz is a senior executive in a marketing company. She has few problems controlling her working time but finds it difficult to balance her long hours in the office with running a home and looking after a family. A year ago she decided to take some pressure off by delegating some of the household chores to a paid helper. First she paid someone else to do the ironing and the cleaning. This arrangement worked very well so she expanded her helper's duties to include collecting the children from school and doing the weekly shopping.

Time is a valuable resource and your attitude to it and the way you use it means the difference between success and failure, fitness and poor health, peace of mind and anxiety or depression.

The activity trap

Poor time managers are often so busy that they simply can't pause to stop and think about how they are actually spending their time and whether or not what they are doing is actually

getting them anywhere. If you let things drift, your activities –
the way you spend your time day in and day out – may actually
be standing in the way of your achieving your goals and
objectives.

> **Bruce** edits a professional journal for software engineers. He believes
> that time management is an attitude or a state of mind, not a formal
> technique or a particular skill. He says that the important thing is to
> know where you are going and then to do something about getting
> there. If you get caught up in firefighting or in solving other people's
> problems, you will lose that focus and drift off course. He delegates
> routine jobs to his team so that he can concentrate on his real
> priorities.

Here are three typical examples of how your activities can act
as barriers between you and your goals and objectives.

❏ *Crisis management*. Rushing from one problem to the next
   and coping with whatever crisis is most pressing is an all
   too common approach for managers who are not in control
   of their time. The trouble with crisis management is that it
   is frequently stressful for everyone involved, it leads to mistakes and poor performance and it damages the image of
   the company in the eyes of its customers and workforce.
   If you spend your time firefighting, you will find it helpful
   to take time out to consider the real purpose of your job,
   and what your priorities should be in relation to this
   purpose. Instead of dealing with problems as they occur,
   you could try identifying the causes of those problems and
   involving others in finding long-term solutions to them.
   Putting more trust in others requires a large investment of
   time at the beginning, but will save you a great deal of time
   in the long run.

❏ *Being at everyone's beck and call*. This problem arises when
   you compulsively look after other people, so that they
   become completely dependent on you and are unable to

take responsibility or make their own decisions. Although you already feel under pressure, you are frequently taken in by pleas for help or by requests for information and advice. You may even find yourself doing parts of other people's jobs if they seem overworked or out of their depth. If you take over other people's problems in this way, the result will be that you will have no time left to work on areas that are a priority for you. You will also be depriving others of opportunities to grow and develop.

The answer, though not an easy one, is to set limits on the extent to which you are prepared to get involved in solving other people's problems. Instead, try to help them to become more independent by giving them responsibility and teaching them new skills. Your role should be to guide and support – rather than to take over at the first sign of trouble.

❏ *Being on a treadmill*. Doing the same things day after day or week after week can make your life easy and quiet, but the work may not be challenging enough and you may feel that you are not getting anywhere. Managers who work on a treadmill are often under stress because of frustration and often feel that their talents are not being recognized and used to the full.

One solution is to get back to basics by clarifying the purpose and responsibilities of your job and seeing how far what you do is actually achieving that purpose. If your current role is not stretching you enough, you could try negotiating an extension of your responsibilities so that what you do will provide you with more challenges and, ultimately, more job satisfaction. Then you need to plan your time carefully so that you are able to make the best use of the opportunities around you for achieving your newly identified objectives.

The activity trap means that we simply carry on doing things out of a misplaced sense of responsibility or out of habit. It means responding to a situation without thinking of the consequences of our actions. The way out of the activity trap is to focus on what we really want to achieve, to decide on our priorities and only then to decide on how to use our time to best effect.

> **Christiana**, a conference organizer, found that she often could not get on with her planning or report writing because of constant phone calls. She then asked her personal assistant to screen her calls so that only the most urgent ones would be switched through to her when she was busy. Now Christiana makes a point of blocking out a short period each day to respond to phone calls.

WHAT IS TIME MANAGEMENT?

There are two sides of better time management: things we wish to do and things we wish to avoid doing.

For example, we might wish to:

❑ use time at work more effectively;
❑ get more things done in the available time;
❑ balance the time we spend at work with more time for ourselves and our families;
❑ feel more relaxed and in control of our time.

Things we wish to avoid might include:

❑ wasting time;
❑ forgetting to do important things;
❑ rushing to meet deadlines;
❑ being late for meetings;
❑ feeling stressed and out of control.

> **Gavin** felt he wanted to take a long hard look at his life because work and family commitments were getting on top of him. He decided that what he wanted from time management was to get rid of the constant anxiety that he was out of control, that he had lost some important papers or that he had forgotten to do something really vital. He also wanted to stop wasting time and to take up some leisure activities with his family.

Your attitude to time

Many of us feel threatened or driven by time. We become anxious about tight deadlines, we are overwhelmed by urgent tasks piling up and, on top of that, we are under increasing pressure to improve our skills and produce better results. The chances are that if we feel like this at work, we will live the rest of our lives at the same breakneck speed, unable to take our eyes off the clock when we are at home with the family or relaxing with friends.

Other people seem able to use time as if it is a resource like any other. Because they know what their priorities are, they are able to plan the best way to allocate their time. These people remain calm and in control, even when unexpected events threaten to send them temporarily off course. The best time managers are those that have a developed a sense of different kinds of time:

❑ the time that they must plan, control and use in the most efficient way possible;

and

❑ the time during which they can be free from the pressure of time.

Are you in control of your time or is it controlling you? Are you able to change your approach to time, depending on what you are doing?

The way you manage your time reflects your attitude to life in general. Accepting that you are in charge of your life and taking responsibility for the way you use your time is the first step to a constructive attitude. The mere fact that you reading this book shows that you have begun to consider making some important changes. One thing is certain – when you begin to manage your time better, you will soon notice important improvements in other aspects of your life.

Barbara started to think about time management when she was a personal assistant in a busy communications company. At that time she had been divorced for five years and was bringing up two children on her own. Her life was extremely busy yet it seemed that, although she was running as fast as could, she was actually going nowhere. When things became critical she asked a close friend to help her plan how she could make changes. Three years later she has been on a management development course and has secured a better paid job in charge of a team of administrative officers. She now makes it a priority to take at least one evening a week to play badminton and have a drink with friends.

By choosing the right things to do and working through them efficiently, you can free up time either for more work or for the things you enjoy. What we are saying is that you can control those aspects of your life to change and which ones you want to keep as they are.

MYTHS ABOUT TIME MANAGEMENT

Before we go any further, let's dispel a few myths about time management. Which of the following have you heard others say, or imply? And, be honest, which ones do you believe in yourself?

❑ *If you are efficient you must be effective too.*

Not true. Being efficient means doing things quickly and correctly – but efficiency in itself will not achieve your objectives. To get the results you and your organization are aiming for, you have to be effective – this means knowing what your priorities are and doing the right things at the right time to bring them about.

❏ *If you want a job done well, do it yourself.*

Not true. Inability or unwillingness to delegate is one of the primary causes of poor performance in business. While your time is taken up doing tasks that are not central to your role and your objectives, you cannot focus on the things that will make a difference to your results. Other people will almost certainly do things differently – but their way may be equally as good if not better than yours.

❏ *There's only one correct way to do a job.*

Not true. It's so easy to get into a rut, but if you can allow yourself the time to step back for a moment you may be able to think how a particular time-consuming task can be done more efficiently and more effectively. You can ask questions like: What is the purpose of the task? What are the desired outcomes? When should it be done? Who should do it? (Does it always have to be the same person?) How should this task be done?

❏ *You don't get good results unless you put a lot of work into a job.*

Not true. The results of a particular job depend on the quality of the work that is put into it, not necessarily the amount of time that you spend on it.

❏ *You can't be productive unless you're busy all the time.*

Not true. If you are a good time manager you can save time for activities like thinking, reading, meeting others and planning future developments. You may not look busy if you are doing research or putting your creative or planning skills to work, but you will certainly be doing the kind of work that is vital to long-term survival and success in business. Some organizations are so convinced of the importance of 'thinking and planning time' that they insist that every manager does this for the first half hour of each working day.

❏ *If you are a careful time manager, there will be no risk, joy or spontaneity in your life.*

Not true. The techniques we look at in this book are there to be used when, where and how *you* want. This could mean, for example, that you might choose to work at peak efficiency only when you really need to – for example in the periods you allocate for working on priority tasks. Although effective time management can help you take control of your own time, this does not mean that you have to remove the spontaneity from your life. Hopefully what it will do is take away the unwanted 'crisis management' and the last minute panic to meet deadlines.

❏ Why you want to manage your time better?

_____

_____

_____

_____

❏ What benefits do you hope this will bring for you?

_____

_____

_____

_____

WHERE DOES THE TIME GO?

Very few people have a true picture of how they spend their time. Many of us think we know what we are doing and for how long, but in reality our memory of how we spend our time is usually wildly inaccurate. So if you are serious about trying to manage your time better, you first need to find out how you are spending your time now and then analyse the results.

Some people are put off the idea of keeping a time log because they think it will be tedious, but in reality you will soon find that it is very revealing. You may even discover that the process of recording what you are doing with your time will in itself be enough to jog you into making subtle changes in your behaviour.

Day	Date			Page no.
Activity/task	Start	Finish	Comments	

You may find it useful to use a format similar to the one above for your own time diary, and a small notebook is ideal for this. Try to complete the diary at regular intervals during the day, rather than wait till last thing at night, by which time you may have forgotten what you did and when. You need to be very disciplined about making your entries – and you will find that the task of completing it becomes less boring after a while. The last point is that it is absolutely vital to be honest – the only person you will be kidding is yourself.

Record everything that you do during the day, not just the time you spend at work.

Once you have kept a time diary for a week, you should spend at least half an hour analysing how you spent your time during the week. Then draw some conclusions from your analysis and take the appropriate action. For example:

❑ If only ten hours out of 40 were spent on an important project, you may like to look at ways of increasing this percentage. How can you cut down on time wasted or on activities that are less important?
❑ If three hours a day are spent dealing with phone interruptions, are there ways in which you can get your calls screened, and then deal with the important ones in batches?
❑ If you spent more than 15 hours a week watching TV, could you cut this down by one-third and do something more active with the time you have saved?

Your life areas

Next, you may find it interesting to follow up the time logging exercise by analysing how you allocate your time between your main life areas. This is a good way of finding out whether you are spending your time in the way that you really want to. Have you got things in balance?

Seven life areas that you may want to look at are:

❑ *paid work*: any work that you do which is paid, either in a job or self-employment;
❑ *home and family*: time that you spend with your partner or your family;
❑ *study*: including going to college or evening classes, studying at home, doing open learning or reading;
❑ *unpaid work*: voluntary work, involvement with the church, political parties or other community groups;

❑ *leisure*: sport and hobbies, television, theatre, cinema, eating out and relaxing with family and friends;
❑ *maintenance*: time you spend taking care of yourself or others or your home;
❑ *sleep*.

Break your time log into the areas that are appropriate for you and then make a bar chart that shows how much time you spent on each area. Don't worry if you are not sure which area one activity should fit into – just put it where it seems to make sense. Figure 1.1 illustrates the following examples:

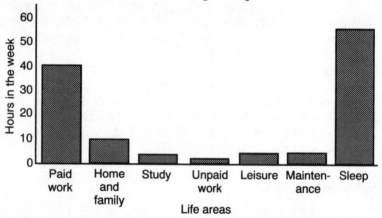

Figure 1.1 *Time spent on the seven life areas*

❑ *paid work*: 40 hours;
❑ *home and family*: 10 hours;
❑ *study*: 3 hours;
❑ *unpaid work*: 2 hours;
❑ *leisure*: 5 hours;
❑ *maintenance*: 5 hours;
❑ *sleep*: 56 hours.

You can now start to consider whether you are allocating your time in the way that you want to. Are you investing it in areas that benefit you, that help you to achieve your goals and move your life forward? Or is your life being dictated to by others?

Do you feel that you spend enough time with your partner or family? Do you make time during the week for physical exercise?

Part of the business of time management is to get the whole of your life in balance – so that you are allocating your time in ways that are important for you. You will find the material in the rest of this book very helpful when you are planning how to improve the way you manage your time – both at work and in the rest of your life.

HOW EFFECTIVELY DO YOU USE YOUR TIME NOW?

Before you start to plan how you are going to get more control over your time, it is important to identify which areas are in most urgent need of attention. Putting the issues into an order of priority and dealing with the most pressing ones first will make your action plan seem far less overwhelming.

Read through the questions and tick yes or no for each one:

Your priorities

1. Are you sure what your main work objectives are? ☐

2. Are you clear about the amount of time you spend on the different areas of your life? ☐

3. Do you know what you want to be doing in one year's time – and in the next three to five years? ☐

4. Do you find it easy to identify which tasks are most important? ☐

5. Do you spend more time than you should doing routine jobs? ☐

6. Do you find that you have enough time to spend on important thinking and planning tasks? ☐

Overload

7. Do you often feel anxious or worried about getting work done? ☐

8. Do you know if you really have too much work to do? ☐

9. Do you always say 'yes' to additional work, even if you are fully loaded? ☐

10. Do you cancel leisure activities in favour of work? ☐

Delegation

11. Do you prefer to do jobs yourself rather than give them to others? ☐

12. Do you see delegation as an important part of your role? ☐

13. Do you plan what and how to delegate well in advance? ☐

14. Are you willing to train and support others while they are learning how to do a task you have delegated? ☐

Planning

15. Do you always know whether you have time spare to fit in any additional work? ☐

16. Do you often take work home or stay very late to finish something? ☐

17. Do you find it impossible to get through all the work you have to do in a day? ☐

18. Are you often late for appointments? ☐

Techniques

19. Do you often put off work till tomorrow? ☐

20. Do you find it difficult to end a conversation? ☐

21. Do you allow people (or phone calls) to interrupt you at any time? ☐

22. Do you feel that meetings often waste your time? ☐

23. Do you have a large pile of reading material to tackle? ☐

There are no right or wrong answers to the questions – the activity has simply helped you to identify the approaches and attitudes that you already find useful and those areas where you may want to develop new behaviours.

The ideal time manager would have answered:

❑ 'yes' to questions 1, 2, 3, 4, 6, 8, 12, 13, 14 and 15;
❑ 'no' to questions 5, 7, 9, 10, 11, 16, 17,18, 19, 20, 21, 22.

Hopefully the quiz has made you realize that you are probably not such a poor time manager as you might have thought! However, it should also have given you some clues about the areas you might find it useful to work on:

❑ If most of your problems are in **Your priorities**, you will find Chapter 2 particularly relevant.
❑ If most of your ticks are in **Overload**, you will find Chapter 3 particularly relevant.
❑ If most of your ticks are in **Delegation**, you will find Chapter 4 particularly relevant.
❑ If most of your ticks are in **Planning**, you will find Chapter 5 particularly relevant.
❑ If most of your ticks are in **Techniques**, you will find Chapter 6 particularly relevant.

SUMMARY

In this chapter you have explored what time management is – and what it is not.

❑ Time is a valuable resource because it is non-renewable; to be an effective manager you need to learn how to manage your time well.

❑ Poor time management may actually be standing in the way of your achieving your goals and objectives.

❑ Accepting that you are in charge of your life and taking responsibility for the way you use your time is the first step to a constructive attitude to time.

❑ Although effective time management can help you take control of your own time, this does not mean that you have to remove the spontaneity from your life.

❑ Keeping a time log will help you to work out where the time is going and how you might be able to make improvements.

In Chapter 2 we shall look at ways of identifying the things that are important in your life – the things that you should be spending your time on.

2

GETTING YOUR PRIORITIES RIGHT

Few people would set out on a journey without knowing where they are heading. Yet this is what so many of us do in our lives, and the result is that we often drift aimlessly, wondering why it is that we feel frustrated and unfulfilled. We are often so busy at home and at work that we don't have time to stop and think why we are not achieving what we want to achieve.

This chapter will help you to identify areas where you may be spending time on things that are not important. It is about finding out what your goals are, so that you can identify your priorities and decide how best to allocate your time.

HOW DO YOU SPEND YOUR TIME?

Before you can start to make better use of your time (which you will be doing in the next chapter) you need to be quite sure of two things:

❑ what you are actually doing with your time at the moment;
❑ how you want to be spending your time after you have acquired and implemented your new time management skills.

We saw in the last chapter that there are four main ways in which our time gets used up:

❑ *We spend our lives dealing with crises and problems.* Some people find it exciting to run from one disaster to another – dealing with equipment that has broken down, pacifying angry customers, finding last minute replacements for staff who are ill, resolving conflicts between team members. But if you are forever picking up the pieces when things have gone wrong, you can't focus on the more positive aspects of your job and your life. Establishing how much time you should be devoting to different areas – planning ahead – will help you to avoid the pitfalls of crisis time management.

❑ *We respond to the demands that others place on us.* In your case it may be your boss, your work team, your colleagues, your customers and your suppliers. If you include friends and family the list of other people who make demands starts to look frighteningly long. If you try to meet all of these demands, not only will you suffer immense stress, you will also lose sight of what it is that you want to do with your life.

❑ *We do things out of habit.* Habits are routines, repeated patterns of behaviour. Human beings are creatures of habit, but if we spend too much of our time doing things out of habit, without thinking about why we are doing them, or whether we need to do them at all, we will fail to make the most of our lives. The trick is to make sure that your habits are helpful rather than unhelpful.

❑ *We can make realistic decisions to use time to achieve our goals.* Once you are aware of your goals, such decisions become much easier. When demands are made on you can decide whether or not to respond, and if so, how much time to allocate to a particular request. You can learn habits that will actually help you get work done and achieve your goals. Being better at managing our time means making sure that we decide how we are going to use our time – and that these decisions get us closer to achieving our goals.

This chapter aims to help you to make sure that most of your activities are in the final category, rather than in the first three.

LIFE PLANNING

To get more in control of your time, you may find it valuable to start by thinking about where you want to go in the next year, the next five years and the next ten years. But first it will help to take stock of your life to date, so that you can start to identify what you have already achieved and begin to look forward to the future.

You can start this process by drawing your lifeline. This is a diagram or graph which represents the highs and the lows of

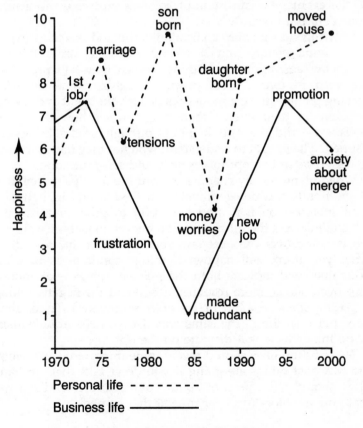

Figure 2.1 *Example of a lifeline*

your life to date – the peaks of achievement and the troughs of failure. It is best to draw two lines to represent your personal life and your studies and working life.

Figure 2.1 shows what your completed chart might look like. Start by putting crosses to represent the level of happiness you achieved as a result of the most important decisions, events and transitions that you have gone through. You might find it easiest to start where you are now and go backwards. Don't rush this activity; once you start thinking back you will start to recall all sorts of significant, but forgotten, events. When you have put in all the events you can think of, join the crosses up to achieve your personal 'lifeline'.

Drawing your lifeline can be a powerful and revealing experience. Some people find it hard because it forces them to remember and think about things which they had previously preferred to forget. Most people recognize some important turning points – the consequences of both the good and the bad decisions in their lives. Others begin to see how they made decisions – did they think things through or did things just happen? They begin to understand whether they have preferred to take risks or just opt for security and self-protection.

When planning any changes in your life it helps to look back at the trends and developments that have been highlighted in your lifeline. You may find it helpful to draw another chart which illustrates the future. Take an honest look at the way your job is going over the next few years. Draw a line to indicate what you think will happen if things continue as they are. Your lines will indicate both the positive things – promotion, improved status, more responsibility – and the negative things – getting stuck in a rut or possible redundancy. Think about your personal life in the same way. Do you see trouble ahead or do things look as if they are on the up?

These future lines should reveal some important truths about the way that things are going if you don't take them in hand. They should tell you a lot about your priorities and the way that you are allocating your time at the moment.

Setting goals

Now you are ready to think about your goals in life – where would you would really like to be next year, in five years' time and in ten years? You could draw up separate lists of goals for your professional and your personal life, but making a combined list will help to ensure that your two lists are compatible. For example, making more money may well prove to conflict with your desire to spend more time with your partner or family.

Your goals can be as generalized or specific as you like at this stage. For example:

❏ I want to earn a lot of money (general).
❏ I would like to become a landscape gardener (specific).
❏ Having a good family life and plenty of close friends is very important for me (general).
❏ I plan to ask a friend to join me on a three-week trip to America (specific).

It is vital to check that your goals are achievable and realistic because the last thing you want to do is to set yourself up to fail. Make sure, for example, that your objectives are within your personal control. For example, if you want to have your boss's job, your success depends on what another person decides to do – and he or she may stick around much longer than you anticipated!

Similarly, make sure that you have got what it takes to fulfil your goals. This is a difficult one because you have to be realistic without underestimating your potential. Don't be too hard on yourself. People don't usually lack the resources to succeed, they may just lack control over those resources.

Finally, look hard at your list of goals and put them in order of priority. None of them will be achieved by luck – they need planning, discipline and sacrifice. You may well have to make some difficult decisions and let some things go if you are to achieve those that are most important to you.

The experience of clarifying your goals will move you on a long way towards taking control of your life. If you focus hard on your goals you will find that you almost subconsciously start to make things happen. By answering the question 'what is really important to me?', you are in a position to apply your motivation, your resources and your time to achieving what you want.

Taking action

Don't stop at simply identifying where you want to be – make your thoughts a reality by planning and taking the relevant action. You can do this by noting down precisely what you will do to achieve the goals that you have already identified. If you want to make a lot of money how are going to achieve this? By starting a business? Buying stocks and shares? Learning a new skill? Will you increase your circle of friends by taking up a hobby, by joining a club or by organizing regular social gatherings or outings? Or do you need to undertake a combination of different activities to achieve your goal?

To manage your time effectively in the medium to long term, it is useful to think about when you intend to carry out each part of your plan. To make sure that you allocate your time effectively, you should give yourself a deadline or a timeframe for achievement of each of the activities you have identified.

TURNING TASKS INTO GOALS

If you don't find it easy to start by making goals, you can attack the problem from the other end. Look at the things you do and decide how each one is helping you to get where you want to go, both in your work and in your private life.

Begin by making a list of all the tasks and responsibilities that take up your time at work. These may include general responsibilities such a managing a budget or more specific tasks like preparing a mail-out or answering the phone. From this list, identify the items that you believe contribute most towards the key purpose of your job. If you do not have a clear, up-to-date job description or specification, now is the time to discuss these matters with your immediate boss or a personnel manager.

Next make your key work goals clear and specific and to each one attach a list of the things that you do in order to achieve it. For example:

1. Effective organization of business resources:
   — arranging finance;
   — recruiting staff;
   — purchasing equipment;
   — allocating duties;
   — introducing new working procedures;
   — and so on.
2. Planning the future development of the business:
   — keeping abreast of changes that are taking place in the industry and the market;
   — finding out about changing customer requirements;
   — seeking ways to increase efficiency and reduce waste;
   — developing new products or new markets for existing products;
   — and so on.

Again, you may need to discuss these aspects with your boss, so that you reach a shared understanding of what you should be aiming for at work and how each of these activities is helping you to achieve these things.

Finally, consider if there is anything you can do to minimize the time you spend on the tasks that do not contribute to your central goals. And how can you make sure that you spend your most productive time on things that relate directly to these?

Do the same thing with your out-of-work activities – you will find the results fascinating and revealing.

GIVING YOURSELF A BREAK

There are many people in the business world who boast that they never take a break during the working day. These same people often work late or take work home – maybe even spending part of the weekend working as well. But, in fact, they are doing themselves and their organizations a disservice because the longer they work without a break, the more their performance will deteriorate. It is a false economy to save time by cutting down on relaxation and leisure activities and it is a mistake to wait till you feel tired before taking a break.

Taking breaks – doing something completely different or simply taking time out to relax – improves the results that you are able to achieve. At certain times the work may be going very well and it may seem tempting to continue for another few minutes or hours, but even then it is still better to take a break. Your mind will remain sharp and creative, and your capacity to take in, integrate and recall pieces of information will improve if you discipline yourself to taking breaks at regular intervals.

It is therefore important to plan and manage your time away from work just as carefully as your working time itself. Don't just tell yourself that you will take a holiday as soon as you have time – treat all your breaks like urgent appointments with yourself, your family or your friends and put them in your diary or planner. You will gain great benefit from arranging your holidays and long weekends well in advance and sticking to your plans no matter what.

But it's not just the longer breaks that need to be carefully programmed into your life. A well planned short break is often a very efficient method of reducing stress and improving your performance. Quality is more important than the amount of time that you spend away from work – so it does not matter if you can only afford a few hours away from your desk. If you take regular breaks, you will not need so long in any case.

How you use this time will determine how valuable it is for you. The important point is to do something different from what you do the rest of the time. If you are on your feet all day dealing with people, you will feel better if you spend your free time relaxing quietly on your own. If, on the other hand, you spend your working life sitting in an office, you will appreciate doing something active in the open air.

CONQUERING THE TYRANNY OF THE URGENT

No matter what we resolve to achieve at the beginning of each day, there's rarely enough time to do it all. By the time the day ends we often feel that we've spent too long on one task and not enough on another. We may have put have put off a really important job till tomorrow, while we paid attention to the more pressing but less important jobs.

This part of the chapter will be useful if you often find it hard to identify the jobs that should be your important priorities and have more time spent on them.

Urgent or important?

It is common for people to find that they spend a large proportion of their time dealing with relatively unimportant but urgent tasks, rather than tackling the tasks that are central to their roles and that will help them to achieve the purpose and objectives of their jobs.

If you are one of those people, you may feel that you spend a great deal of your time responding to other people's demands, rather than accomplishing the tasks that are your personal priorities. This is certain to leave you with a sense of being controlled by time, rather than feeling that you can use time as one of the resources that will help you to achieve your objectives.

Martia is a senior occupational therapist in a health service trust. She firmly believes that it is vital to know what her key tasks are because otherwise there is a danger of simply reacting to other people and events. She has found life much easier since the staff appraisal system was introduced because this has helped to clarify the areas on which she should be concentrating her attention.

One way of confronting this problem is to recognize the difference between urgent tasks (those that have to be completed by a fixed deadline) and important tasks (those that will have a large or long-term effect on something you value).

Unfortunately, it is easy to confuse urgency with importance when you are identifying your priorities. Superficially, a report that is expected this afternoon seems more important than the forecast for next year's production targets, which is not required till the end of the month. But if the report is not central to your work goals, it must take a lower priority than the forecast, which does contribute to your key job purpose. You might therefore decide to ask someone else to write the report or to spend only a short time preparing it.

Plotting tasks on a grid like the one below helps to separate importance and urgency:

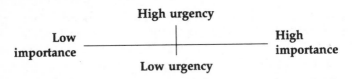

Using the grid can help you to work out the relative urgency of different tasks. You are then in a position to complete the most urgent tasks before the least urgent ones. The grid also enables you identify which tasks deserve extra time and care because they are more important.

This 'time management grid' is a very useful way of analysing the demands on your time. Whether they are demands which other people are making on you or demands you are making on yourself, they can be evaluated in terms of their importance and their urgency.

What makes a job more important?

You need to be aware that many factors can change to make a task more important and move to the right of the grid. Things move fast in the business world, and you need to be aware of how changes in the external environment and in the organization itself can affect the relative importance of the things you have to do. The vital point is to remember that your analysis of what is important at work is unlikely to remain static for long.

Although you are the only person who can decide about the priorities you should give to the demands on your time, don't forget that these priorities affect other people. At work, of course, any changes you wish to make in the pattern of your daily activities must be discussed with your boss. But in other areas of your life you also need to be aware of the implications for those around you of the decisions you make.

What makes a job more urgent?

For example, a job has been lying on your desk for a week. When it first came in you decided that it was a 'low urgency/ low importance' job and that you had more important things to do. As the days passed, the job gradually became more urgent. Now it has to be done before lunchtime and has become an urgent priority. However, the *importance* of the job has not changed; the passage of time usually makes a task more urgent, but not more important.

Using the quadrants

As you have seen, the time management grid is composed of four squares or quadrants:

❑ *The top left-hand square* contains a note of the jobs that are fairly urgent but relatively low in importance. These things tend to get done immediately because they are pressing, but the problem is that people usually spend too much time on them. Ideally, you should deal with demands in this square as quickly as possible.

❑ *The bottom left-hand square* contains the tasks that are neither important nor urgent. The danger is that you may waste too much time doing these things because they are easy or because you enjoy doing them. As a general rule it is often better to leave these things until they become a little more urgent – especially if there are more important things to do. You should spend as little time as possible attending to the jobs that appear in this square.

❏ *The top right-hand square* incorporates the tasks that are both urgent and important. The danger is that these tasks don't get the time and attention that they deserve because they are dealt with in a last-minute rush. You may need to delegate or put off less important things if you want to make enough time for this group of tasks.

❏ *The bottom right-hand square* includes the tasks that are important but not urgent. These may have a deadline that is a long way in the future or they may have no deadline at all. The danger here is that you may put off doing them because they are not urgent, or you may never do them. If there is a deadline, the jobs will gradually become more and more urgent until they enter the top right-hand quadrant. You will then have to apply crisis management to get them done.

High urgency

In here write the jobs which are urgent but not important *How can you avoid spending too much time on jobs in this square?*	Write the demands which are both urgent and important. *How can you make sure there is enough time to do these jobs well?*
Write the things which are low in importance but are not urgent. *How can you avoid the temptation to do these easy jobs when you should be spending time on something else?*	Write the things which are not urgent, but which are important. *How can you avoid putting these jobs off because they are not urgent?*

Low importance (left) **High importance** (right)

Figure 2.2 *Time management grid*

Try making a time management grid on a separate piece of paper and jotting down all the activities that you expect to undertake tomorrow or next week, as in shown in Figure 2.2. Once you have worked out their relative importance and urgency, you can start to plan how to avoid the traps that are inherent in each of the quadrants.

Good time managers spend a lot of time on jobs in the bottom right-hand square because it contains the jobs that will have a long-term effect on the development of their organizations, departments or teams.

SUMMARY

In this chapter you have been deciding which of your activities will help you to achieve your goals and which will not.

❑ Drawing a lifeline is useful because this represents the highs and the lows of your life to date – the peaks of achievement and the troughs of failure. You can see how you have spent your time up till now and identify whether significant things happened to you by accident or as a result of a positive decision.

❑ You can draw a line to represent the future as you now see it – this should reveal some important truths about the way that things are going if you don't take them in hand.

❑ Once you have analysed the past, you can set some achievable and realistic goals for the future. Setting goals that are unrealistic or depend on other people's actions can be a recipe for failure.

❑ The experience of clarifying your goals will move you on a long way towards taking control of your life – and your time.

❑ If you don't find it easy to set goals, you can start by looking at the things you do and deciding how each one is helping you to get where you want to go, both in your work and in your private life.

❑ It is just as important to plan your breaks – your time away from work and from domestic duties – as it is to plan your

Continued on next page

working time itself. You can't be an effective manager if you spend all your time working.

❑ The time management grid is a system for differentiating between those tasks which are important and those which are simply urgent.

❑ Good time managers spend a lot of time on jobs in the bottom right-hand square of the quadrant (high importance and low urgency) because it contains the jobs that will have a long-term effect on the development of their organization, department or team.

In the next chapter you will look at ways of using the information that you have gained here to plan how to use your time effectively.

3

PLANNING HOW TO USE YOUR TIME

In the last chapter we saw that it is useful to make decisions about how to use our time on the basis of the relative importance and urgency of particular tasks. This information will put you in a position where you are able to plan how to best use your time to achieve your goals and objectives.

Planning is a vital element of time management. You are more likely to be effective in your work and your private life if you have thought carefully about when tasks should be done, in what order and how long to spend on each one.

PLANNING TOOLS AND TECHNIQUES

Most time managers would be lost without their filofaxes, their diaries or their electronic organizers. The main purpose of such tools is to facilitate planning and to make plans easy to access and to bring up to date.

Betty is a radio producer who has used a filofax to help her improve her time management. Each week she makes a list of the jobs that she has to do and tries to put them into order of priority. Once she has planned how long it will take her to do each task, she allocates a 'slot' for it in her diary. Some of the less important tasks don't go into the diary, they go onto a separate list called 'chores' and get attended to when she has slack time or when she needs a break from the high priority items.

Many of us carry on using the same type of diary or planner year after year, but it is worth reviewing your requirements from time to time to see if some other type of system may suit your needs better. For example, if you have always planned your time on a week-by-week basis, would you find it useful to take a longer-term view? Try looking at your annual, quarterly or even monthly targets and then planning which activities have to be done (when and in what sequence) in order to achieve these. Setting defined goals and translating these into programmes for action are made easier if you use a long-term planning tool like a wall chart or an activity schedule.

On the other hand, you may be the sort of person who takes a long-term view – but finds it difficult to fit in the smaller jobs like making phone calls, buying birthday presents or working out your expenses claim. You may find an electronic system with built-in reminders more useful than a traditional paper-based diary.

Use any planning aids that you find helpful, but make sure that the tool doesn't take over from the essential business of controlling and scheduling time. The tools that are there to help you (but not to enslave you) include:

❑ diaries and planners;
❑ wall charts;
❑ bring-forward systems;
❑ list systems;
❑ schedules and Gannt charts.

A multitude of software packages now provide 'foolproof' time management systems. Many of these are very effective, especially for project management and ensuring that different individuals' activities are coordinated. However, they are not so good for personal day-to-day time planning and, of course, they are not so easy to transport and access as ordinary diaries.

DIARIES AND PLANNERS

Diaries are essential planning tools. They can be used to record:

❑ your own activities and appointments (including appointments with yourself to do certain important things);
❑ activities and appointments of your colleagues – these could be entered in a different colour pen, or in a column of their own, to avoid confusion;
❑ periodic or routine tasks and anniversaries;
❑ action points or 'to do' lists for the day or week – prioritized and then crossed through when completed;
❑ any tasks that have been postponed or carried forward – these can be noted as reminders so that you don't forget them.

There are many types of diary to choose from, including those that you print out yourself from a computer package or those that you buy ready printed from the stationer's or office equipment supplier. Think carefully about your ideal diary format and page layout. You may require a week to a page, a week spread over two pages or a whole month on one large page that can be folded out. You may want to a line for every hour or every half hour, or you may prefer lots of unmarked rules so that you can write as much or as little as you need to.

Electronic systems

An electronic diary is a software package for a desktop computer. It allows you to create as many different diaries as you need and then enter details of appointments, reminders, priorities and other information, much as you would on a paper diary page.

Some advantages of electronic diaries are that they can:

❑ be programmed not to accept appointments on specific days;
❑ flash up reminders of appointments;
❑ cross refer items;
❑ accept unrestricted amounts of text.

When the diary holder is away from the office, he or she can check on any changes to the diary by linking a portable computer up to the office computer via the telephone line. When computers are networked, people can access each other's diaries to find free times to book meetings. With many systems it is now possible to get the computer to search and cross match times for meetings.

Visual planners

Visual planners can range from big 'year to a view' wall charts to weekly or yearly planners in a personal organizer or diary. Although these planners can also be computerized, a simple chart drawn up on a whiteboard will often do the job. If you prefer, you can use proprietary devices like a pegboards or other types of boards with tapes, flags or stickers.

The emphasis is on quick reference and seeing how one activity fits in with others by using different shaped and coloured symbols to represent specific people or events. However, a visual planner is not appropriate for detailing all appointments because there isn't enough space and because too much detail confuses the broad picture. There are many different styles of planner; before buying one it is important to think about what you really need it to do.

Bring-forward systems

Sometimes tasks you have scheduled in your diary or on your wall planner have to be postponed. If this happens, you need to remind yourself that the tasks are still waiting to be done. This is where a bring-forward system is essential.

These are two of the best known bring-forward systems:

❑ *Diary.* You simply make a note of the task to be brought forward at the appropriate day in the diary or electronic system. If the diary is a paper one, you could slot letters or other documents relating to the task at the appropriate day or week. In this way you have all the information you need to carry out the task at the appointed time

❏ *Concertina file*. These are cardboard files that are segmented into separate compartments and often labelled 1 to 31 for the days of the month. They are used in exactly the same way as a diary, putting in a copy of a letter or a note to remind you what is to be done that day. When the day arrives, you take them out and act on the reminders.

THE LIST SYSTEM

One of the commonest and most valuable of all planning tools is the 'to do' list. This system can help you to plan on a week-by-week or a day-by-day basis. It is good practice to get into the habit of making a list at certain times each day – first thing in the morning or last thing before going home are often good times. Once you have made your list you will have to decide:

❏ in what order you will tackle the items on your list;
❏ how long you will spend on each item.

Jill is a hard pressed export sales manager who has had years of experience of trying to fit 12 hours' work into an eight-hour day. One of her secrets is to break large jobs down into smaller, more achievable tasks. The tasks can then be viewed as a sequence of steps which she can tackle one by one at pre-set times. Breaking a task down into its component parts provides an excellent spring-board for achieving something that may have seemed quite overwhelming at first. In this way, she doesn't feel that she has to devote a whole day or maybe a whole week to one time-consuming job. She can do it bit by bit, fitting the smaller tasks in with the million and one other things that she has to do.

Order planning

Some items on the list will have a fixed deadline, for example a report which is due by a certain time on a certain day. Other items will have a natural deadline. For example, if you want one of your team to do a different job from the usual one today, you will need to speak to him or her first thing in the morning.

Once you have taken out those things which have a fixed deadline or a natural deadline there will still be some tasks left on the list. You should then be prepared to make decisions about the order in which to do these things on the basis of their urgency and their importance. It is a good idea to do the urgent things first, making sure that you have left time to do the things which are important but not urgent. A part of the day that is usually quiet would be a good time to devote to any important task which requires concentration.

There are two great dangers to avoid when order planning:

❑ you may do things in a certain order out of habit;
❑ you may do the small or pleasant things first.

As we have seen, the problem is that if you spend too long on the tasks that are easy and urgent, you may put off or never get round to doing the ones that are difficult, unpleasant and important.

Anita is a personnel manager who finds that the most difficult part of time management is making a start on the things that she finds daunting. Once she has actually done something, she often finds that the task isn't nearly as bad as she thought it was going to be. Having made a start, she might then break off for an hour or so to tackle a couple of small admin jobs or make a phone call or two. After that it's not nearly so bad going back to the bigger task.

Allocating time

The next step is to estimate how long each item on your ordered list will take. This is very difficult, but essential because failing to make a correct estimate of the time involved in each job or part of a job is the most common reason for managers failing to meet their deadlines.

The only way to do this is to make an estimate based on your past experience. You may be proved wrong in the end, but it is important to make some sort of informed guess. Having made your time estimates, you may want to reconsider the order in which you will do things. For instance, there may be more time towards the end of the day to complete a task you had originally put high on your list of things to do.

When you have finished your planning you may find that you have 16 hours of work in an eight-hour day! If this is the case, at least you know in advance that you are unlikely to get everything done in the time unless you reorganize your work or get some help.

Coping with the unexpected

There are bound to be days when what you have planned to do does not go well. These are the sorts of things that can happen to upset your plans:

❑   there is an accident;
❑   machinery or equipment breaks down;
❑   someone asks you to do something extra.

Coping with accidents

If someone in your team has an accident, you may well be forced to abandon your plans completely for the day. Accidents can be extremely costly in terms of human suffering, time spent dealing with the aftermath, lost productivity and poor public image, so it is worth spending time on:

❏ reducing the possibility of accidents happening in the first place;
❏ planning what you would do if an accident did occur.

The first thing is, of course, to take steps to reduce the likelihood of accidents happening. There are two main reasons why accidents and injuries happen in the workplace:

❏ the environment or working conditions are unsafe;
❏ people behave in an unsafe manner.

These are often called 'primary' causes because they can lead directly to injuries or damage to property. The important point is that if you aware of these different types of primary causes, you are more likely to be able to take action before things actually go wrong. You can eliminate or reduce the risk of accidents if you monitor the working environment regularly and systematically and make sure that people have all the information and training that they require.

If, despite all your efforts, accidents do happen, you should have your contingency plans ready so that you are able to move into action straight away. For example:

❏ Who are the trained first aiders in your section?
❏ Which doctor is your organization registered with?
❏ Where is the nearest accident/emergency unit?
❏ What procedures have to be followed in the event of an accident?
❏ Who has to be informed?
❏ How will you go about investigating an accident?

Finally, it is important to reduce the disruption an accident has on the work of the department or team. No matter how you feel, you must inspire confidence in others by following the procedures as calmly and carefully as possible and by being seen to take steps to prevent such a thing happening again. You may need to be prepared to swap duties around or to draft in a replacement so that there is cover for the injured person.

Machinery/equipment breakdown

If breakdowns are regular time wasters, it is worth thinking about what you can do to reduce the time lost on a long-term basis. The time management rules here are the same as those for dealing with accidents. In other words, first try to avoid breakdowns happening in the first place; then be ready to deal with them if they do happen.

Can you:

❑ press for more regular servicing of machines and equipment?
❑ make a case for buying new ones?
❑ arrange a system so that engineers or breakdown staff arrive as quickly as possible?
❑ make sure everyone knows exactly what to do if a breakdown occurs?

It is estimated that one company in every 500 suffers a major computer failure each year. Companies who are dependent on computer-based information systems will go under if they suffer a major system failure and have neglected to arrange for adequate backup.

Bob is a production manager in a light engineering factory. His approach is to turn a disaster into an opportunity to show what the team can do. He always tries to stay calm and to stop and think before deciding on a way forward. It often helps to talk to others who are closely involved or who have experienced such a problem before.

Someone asks you to do something extra

What happens if you have drawn up your plan for the day and along comes your boss, a colleague or a customer with other ideas about how you ought to spend your time?

If this is a common problem for you, once again you should

take steps to reduce the likelihood of it happening and to reduce the disruption when it does. Planning your day or your week in advance enables you to know how much (if any) spare time you have available. Knowing the relative importance and urgency of each of your tasks will also help you to be aware of the likely effects of taking on extra work. All of these facts are crucial if you want to be able to negotiate the extra workload with the person concerned.

If you do have to fit someone else's requirements into your day, you can return to your original time plan when the other matter has been dealt with. At this stage you will have to replan the remainder of the day's activities based on a review of goals for the day and a quick reassessment of your priorities and goals. You will not achieve what you originally set out to achieve but at least you will still feel in control.

Remember that you have a right to set a limit on the work you do, and to refuse unreasonable requests.

MAKING AND USING A SCHEDULE

A schedule is a type of action plan that may be used for long- or medium-term projects involving several people. A schedule helps you to work out what steps are required to complete the project, who will take responsibility for each step and when each one will be completed.

Here are the main stages in the preparation of a schedule for a small project.

1. Define the objectives and the desired outputs of the project and specify the key deadlines to be incorporated.
2. Identify the staff and other resources that need to be involved. If possible, call a meeting of those people and carry out steps 3 to 5 below.
3. List all the tasks needed to complete the project and place them in a logical sequence of operation. Notice groupings and links between tasks (for example, Task B cannot start before Task A is complete but C can run parallel to A and B).

Estimate how long each task should take.
5. Prepare a draft chart based on:
   — the list of tasks;
   — the sequence of and relationship between tasks;
   — how long each task should take;
   — the required completion date.
6. After the meeting draw up a formal schedule which shows:
   — the tasks in the order in which they are to be carried out;
   — when they are to be performed and how long is allowed;
   — who is responsible for each task.

Task	By whom	By when
Fix date for course	JM and DS	End of week 1
Agree the budget	JM and DS	End of week 1
Find out how many will attend	DS	End of week 1
Research possible venues	BF	End of week 1
Plan programme for the day	JM	End of week 1
Agree venue	JM and DS	End of week 2
Book venue	BF	End of week 2
Agree programme	JM and DS	End of week 2
Invite speakers	BF	End of week 2
Brief speakers	JM	End of week 3
Prepare visual aids and handouts	JM and BF	End of week 4
Check equipment and materials	JM	End of week 5
Run through	JM	End of week 5

7. Issue copies to all participants with their contributions high-lighted, and ask individuals to report back as they carry out their allocated tasks.

It is important to be aware that some 'slippage' is inevitable, for example through staff sickness, and to build in space for unexpected events. There is an example for a manually produced activity schedule for the planning of a training day on page 53. The event is to take place in six weeks' time.

Gantt Charts

Gantt charts display planned or actual progress against a horizontal timescale as shown in Figure 3.1. As well as showing when various tasks are due to begin and end, Gantt charts can identify the 'critical' links in a project. These are the points at which certain activities must be completed before others can start. If any of these critical activities is delayed, the whole project will be put back.

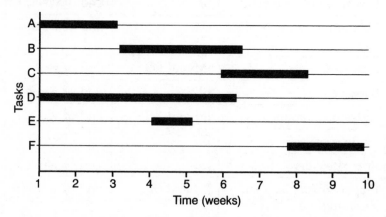

Figure 3.1 *Example of a Gantt chart*

Wendy is a contract caterer who frequently prepares food for weddings and parties for 50, 200 or even 300 people. There is so much to do and to organize, and she also has to coordinate the work of a team of cooks, assistants, waiters and waitresses. If she is not careful, people are wasting time waiting for a particular stage to be complete before they can start to do their bit. Without planning, they would not have the ingredients or equipment that they need and they could easily find themselves with about ten dishes half prepared and nothing finished.

Wendy's planning has to involve the whole team, so that everyone knows what they are expected to do and when. They have to decide on the menu, what they need to buy, how best to organize the shopping, how long each dish will take to prepare and dovetail the preparation so that time is not wasted waiting for things to cook or to set. Things rarely go exactly according to plan but at least they avoid the feeling of total chaos that they have suffered in the past!

MONITORING THE PLAN

It's not enough just to make a plan at the start of a time period or project. You need to build in some time for monitoring, so that you will know whether the plan is working out as you hope or whether it is going off course. When planning your day or your project, therefore, mark in some time to stop and review how well you are doing. This is a good opportunity to make a note of how long things actually took – as compared with your original estimate.

If you are way over time, you can revise your plan by, for example:

❑ making an effort to do things a little quicker for the remainder of the day or project;
❑ cutting out some of the less essential activities;

❑ asking one or more other people to help with certain tasks;
❑ revising the timescale and deadline for completion of the plan.

Make note of any problems that you have encountered with the plan so that you can learn from this experience the next time you carry out a similar exercise. With experience, you will be able to improve on your time estimates and your judgement about people's capabilities.

SUMMARY

This chapter has discussed ways of planning how to use your time to best effect.

❑ It is valuable to review the planning aids that you are using from time to time, to ensure that these are continuing to meet your needs.

❑ Diaries and electronic systems can be used to record your appointments and any time that you want to block out to carry out important tasks. Electronic diaries have a number of advantages over paper ones but they are less easily accessible and less flexible.

❑ Wall charts and visual planners are useful for quick reference and for seeing how one activity fits in with others in the context of whole months or years.

❑ 'To do' lists can help you to plan on a week-by-week or a day-by-day basis. Once you have made your list you decide in what order you will tackle the items on your list and how long you will spend on each item.

❑ To stay in control you have to be ready to cope with the unexpected when putting your 'to do' list into action. It's important to try to prevent disasters from happening and to have some contingency plans ready if they do occur.

❑ Schedules and Gantt charts are tools that will help you to plan how much time to spend on the different stages of

Continued on next page

---

projects. These tools will also help you decide how to sequence the tasks that you have identified.

The focus of the next chapter is overload: how you know if you have too much work to do and how to deal with overload if you feel it is a problem for you.

4

DEALING WITH OVERLOAD

Everyone feels they have too much work to do at some time or another, but constantly having too much to do will eventually lower your performance level. It can also cause a deterioration in your health and can adversely affect your relationships and your family life. If overload is your problem, you will need to discuss this with your manager – you have the right to speak out if you can't cope with what the organization seems to expect.

However, working long hours is not necessarily a sign that you are overloaded with work. It can mean that you need to develop your time management skills. This is why you will find it useful to try some of the techniques suggested in this book before tackling your manager head on. If, however, you really are overloaded, this chapter will help you to decide what to do about it.

HAVE YOU REALLY GOT TOO MUCH WORK?

Long working hours do not necessarily mean you have too much work to do – it could be a reflection of working inefficiently, not recognizing the most important jobs or allowing other people to exploit your good nature. On the other hand, it is of course possible that there is nothing wrong with the way you are managing your time. You may simply have too much work to do in the time available.

Overload often occurs as a result of the combination of roles that people have to perform in their lives, as this case study illustrates.

> *Elizabeth* is an accounts manager in a small advertising agency. Although she finds that she can just about keep on top of her working responsibilities, her overload occurs when she gets home and finds she has to carry out all the housekeeping and child care duties too.
>
> Instead of being able to come home after a stressful day and have a quiet meal and put my feet up, I have to think about the shopping, cooking, cleaning up, helping with homework, getting the kids to bed and preparing clothes for the next day. Then I have to get up at the crack of dawn the next day to get them off to school and make sure that I arrive at work feeling ready for anything.
>
> She is convinced that it is most important for working mothers to negotiate with their partners and children how chores can be shared out more evenly. It is all too common for women to keep on doing most of the chores, even though they resent the situation and end up having little time to relax.

The short quiz below will help you to work out if you are genuinely overloaded with work.

Do you:

- ❏ know what your work goals are and are able to tackle tasks in order of priority? ☐
- ❏ know how your tasks will contribute to your work goals? ☐
- ❏ work out what you have to do – and in what order – on a weekly or daily basis? ☐
- ❏ estimate how long it will take to complete a task before you start it? ☐
- ❏ know how many hours a week you will have to work in order to achieve your goals? ☐
- ❏ delegate as much work as possible to other people? ☐

- [ ] get on with jobs without delay once it is time to start them? [ ]
- [ ] keep telephone interruptions to a minimum? [ ]
- [ ] discourage unscheduled visits? [ ]
- [ ] stop for lunch and other short breaks during the day? [ ]
- [ ] spend a reasonable amount of time on leisure or social activities? [ ]
- [ ] share out household tasks with other members of the family? [ ]

If you already do most of the above and still have too much to do, it is likely that you have a genuine overload.

If, however, you already practise less than three of them, it may be that you need to explore one or two of the time management techniques that we discuss in later chapters of this book. This should help you to judge whether or not you have a real overload.

WHAT TO DO ABOUT THE OVERLOAD

If you are convinced that you have too much work to do, you should understand that you are not alone. Stress and overwork are very common in the late 1990s, as this piece of research illustrates.

Stress in the public services

Research carried out by the Institute of Management among a sample of 2500 managers working in the public services revealed some startling facts and figures:

- [ ] 75 per cent of respondents saw their workload as increasing by up to one-third;
- [ ] 82 per cent said their work was a source of satisfaction;
- [ ] 71 per cent described work as stressful;
- [ ] 70 per cent believed that their overall health was affected by job-related anxiety;

Continued on next page

❏ 66 per cent suffered disturbed sleep;
❏ about 50 per cent said they were unable to get a particular worry out of their head.

Sometimes we feel flattered when people give us extra responsibilities or the opportunity to lead an exciting new project. Then, when the workload seems to be overwhelming, our reaction is often that we are at fault because we are not able to cope. The solution is to resolve to stop being a victim of overwork and to take positive actions to get back in control of what we are doing.

The first step is to recognize and acknowledge how we feel about the overload and the stance we want to take. We may, for instance, feel that we are willing to put in some extra effort for the time being because we are ambitious and want to impress the boss!

It's not easy to work out how you feel about having too much work to do, so you might find it useful to talk this over with a sympathetic colleague. This is what others have thought about being overloaded with work. Do any of these remarks reflect your own feelings?

I feel angry and put on when I have to stay on and work in the evenings. My boss doesn't seem to understand how much I have to do already and he's always giving me more things to do.

I can put up with a bit of extra work from time to time – but I expect my boss to recognize that I must be allowed to take time off when things are slack.

I'm afraid that, if I don't accept the extra projects and tasks with a smiling face, people will think that I'm inefficient and not able to cope. Actually, I think I am quite efficient, but I'm not Superman!

Last week I was asked to lead a team of six who will be tackling an exciting new project over the next few months. I haven't really got the time to do it comfortably, but this is a golden opportunity to gain experience in a new field and I can't afford to miss it.

I can't complain about having too much to do – I know this would jeopardize my chances of gaining promotion. This firm would tell me to get out of the kitchen if I can't stand the heat.

Identifying your feelings will help you to draw up a plan of action. If you end up choosing to do nothing about your heavy workload, at least you will know why you have decided to take this stance. Here are some of the things you can do once you have identified your feelings about your workload:

❑ negotiate your overload;
❑ say 'no' to additional work;
❑ do nothing, but change how you feel about the overload.

Your rights

To put any of these options into practice you first have to believe that you have some basic human rights. These rights are not new or revolutionary – in fact they may seem quite ordinary at first glance. But many of us get so tied up with wanting to do a good job or simply with keeping a hard-won job that we forget that we have rights as well as responsibilities at work. Reminding yourself of these rights will be of particular help if you decide to set a limit on the amount of work you are prepared to do.

❑ You have the right to express your own feelings and opinions about your work.
❑ You have the right to state your own needs about work.
❑ You have the right to place reasonable limits on the amount of work you are prepared to do.
❑ You have the right to refuse people when they make unreasonable demands on your time.
❑ You have the right to expect to be involved in determining the nature and the quantity of work that you will do.
❑ You have the right to be treated with respect as an intelligent and equal person.

For its part, your employer has a moral and legal responsibility to provide a 'safe system of work' – and Health and Safety legislation draws no distinction between physical and mental well-being, as this case illustrates.

Overload in the social services

W, a manager in a social service department, dealt with child abuse cases. The pressure was intense and he suffered a nervous breakdown in 1986. He had no history of mental disorder and had a supportive family. It was agreed that upon his return, W would receive assistance. When he did return he faced a backlog and the agreed assistance did not materialize. As a result he had a second breakdown and he retired. The court held that employers could be liable for foreseeable psychiatric harm resulting from a failure to provide a safe system of work. After the first breakdown, the employer should have taken steps to alleviate the pressure. The council was not judged to be at fault for the first breakdown.

But it may never come down to a legal battle – employers can be reasonable and will often listen to your point of view if you express it calmly and politely. Most bosses who are worth their salt will respond to a reasoned argument from you. It may be that your boss simply does not realize how much you have on your plate and will be grateful when you take the initiative to explain your problems. Remember that it is in your employer's interests as well as your own to make sure that you are able to give of your best.

NEGOTIATING YOUR WORKLOAD

If you have clarified your own feelings and are sure that you really are overloaded, you may then decide to try to negotiate a reduction in your workload. This will be difficult for you if you have never questioned the demands of your boss or your organization before. However, if you are chronically overloaded, this is likely to lead to tiredness, stress and poor performance, so you may be forced to do what you can to improve the situation.

There are two main situations in which you may want to negotiate your workload:

❑ negotiating over a specific piece of work or project;
❑ negotiating your overall workload.

If you are an inexperienced negotiator, you will find it easier to start by discussing a specific piece of work, with the longer-term aim of negotiating your whole workload.

The following guidelines will help you to conduct a successful negotiation:

❑ Decide what you want to achieve as a result of the negotiation and specify your objectives as precisely as possible. 'Delegating the routine filing to the office junior' or 'Taking on a part-time administrative assistant' are much better objectives than the more generalized one of 'Reducing my workload'.
❑ Prepare your evidence – hard facts are always much more convincing than mere opinions or an emotive appeal. If you can produce a time log or a plan of how you intend to spend your time over the next few days, this will be so much the better. Such documents will help you prove that you are much too heavily committed and that you need to reduce your workload.
❑ Work out your fallback position. How far are you prepared to compromise if necessary? Successful negotiations always end with both parties feeling that they have gained something. So if you are to win at least something of what you want, you may have to be prepared to give something away.
❑ Think carefully about what your boss's objectives will be. Trying to see the issue from the other point of view will help you to understand his or her problems. This in turn will help you prepare your responses to any objections.

Finally, choose the time and place of the negotiation carefully. You will have much more chance of success if you choose a relaxed atmosphere and a time when you and your boss will not be interrupted. If you are not too confident about the negotiation, ask a friend to run through it with you. Like all skills, successful negotiation takes practice, so don't expect to be a brilliant performer straightaway.

SAYING 'NO' TO MORE WORK

Your second option is to try to find ways of coping with what work you have and to say 'no' to any additional pieces of work. The problem is that many of us feel so guilty about saying 'no' that we do so indirectly or without conviction. But a firm refusal does not have to be heavy or hurtful; you can speak calmly and still acknowledge the other person's needs and feelings, even while you are saying 'no'.

Many people find it difficult to refuse requests because they hold some of the following beliefs. Which, if any, do you agree with?

❑   Others will be hurt or angry if I refuse their requests.   ☐
❑   People won't like me if I say 'no'.   ☐
❑   It's rude and selfish to say 'no'.   ☐
❑   If I say 'no', other people might start refusing *my* requests.   ☐
❑   Other people's needs are more important than mine.   ☐
❑   Saying 'no' to little things means you are small-minded.   ☐

If you believe any of these myths, you will probably have difficulty in making clear statements of refusal. You are likely to:

❑   say 'yes' when you want to say 'no';
❑   say 'yes' and then feel angry or guilty;
❑   say 'no' but back it up with a string of irrelevant excuses.

To make sure others know that you mean 'no', it is important to learn some new habits. Here are some tactics that you can try:

❑   If you find it difficult to say 'no' straightaway, ask for time to decide. If you agree to something without thinking through the consequences, you may kick yourself later.

❏ Practise saying 'no' without excessive apology or excuses. You can explain why you are saying 'no' without appearing to feel guilty about this.

❏ Once you have said 'no', don't prolong the conversation, you may be tempted to start apologizing or to give in.

❏ Tell the other person how you feel. By saying, 'I feel bad about this but . . .' or 'This is difficult . . .' can reassure the other person that you are not being hostile.

Sticking to your guns

Like most skills worth learning, saying 'no' takes time and practice. But it gets easier the more convinced you become of the benefits of this way of responding. People will soon stop taking advantage of you if they know that you will only accept more work when you genuinely feel that you have enough time to do it properly.

One of the most important lessons to learn is that you must stick to your guns if your refusal is met with renewed efforts to persuade you to say 'yes'. At this point it is vital to repeat your answer calmly until you are sure that it has been understood by the person concerned. It helps to listen carefully to what the other person has to say and acknowledge that he or she has said it.

I appreciate that you need the sales forecast by tomorrow morning but I can't work overtime tonight.

I understand that the accounts have to be prepared immediately but I already have three urgent jobs that have to be completed today.

I can see your problem but, as you can see from my timetable, I don't have time free till next week.

The advantage of repeating the other person's statement is that it helps you to maintain a calm, steady position and communicates the idea that you are really determined. While you are fielding the other person's responses, don't allow yourself to be sidetracked or to become involved in an argument.

Body language

So far we have been talking about the words you should use when refusing a request to do more work. But the right words on their own are not enough; you must also consider the effects of your tone of voice and your body language. For example, if you smile out of nervousness or embarrassment when you are saying 'no', people may think that you mean quite the opposite.

We are all experts in body language because we use it and interpret it every day. The trick is to become aware of ways in which your body language will help to communicate what you want to say to other people.

Avoid these behaviours because they may convey uncertainty or lack of resolve:

❏ allowing your voice to trail off at the end of a sentence;
❏ putting your hand over your mouth when you speak;
❏ looking down at the floor or to one side while talking to someone.

Avoid these behaviours because they may convey aggression or anger:

❏ wagging or pointing your finger;
❏ putting your hands on your hips and leaning forward;
❏ using a 'clipped' voice.

By using the correct body language, you will convince people that you are determined to say 'no' but that you are prepared to talk and listen to other points of view. Try out some of the following:

❏ an open and relaxed posture;
❏ relaxed eye contact;
❏ an upright (but not too rigid) stance.

CHANGING HOW YOU FEEL

The third option when dealing with overload is to do nothing and simply to change how you feel about it. You may choose do this because you recognize that there are good reasons why you will have to put up with the situation as it is. For example:

❑ you are ambitious and want to impress your boss with your ability to cope well under pressure;

❑ you are on a short-term contract and need the experience and the income that this job provides;

❑ everyone else in the department or team is as overworked as you are – so you can't pass your excess work over to anyone else.

But remember that it's not your fault that there is too much work to do – it has happened as a result of someone else's inefficiency or because of the organization's lack of resources. If certain things don't get done at all, this is because you have decided that other tasks must take priority, not because you are incompetent.

If you are prioritizing your work and coping as efficiently as possible with the most important jobs, you can justly feel proud that you have the ability to manage a difficult situation very well.

SUMMARY

The aim of this chapter has been to help you to deal with the problem of overload.

❑ If you find that you have to work long hours, this does not necessarily mean that you are a poor time manager. It could be that you have too much to do in the time available.

❑ If you have explored a number of time management techniques and still have too much to do, you are probably overloaded with work.

Continued on next page

❑ Before you decide what to do about the overload, you first have to clarify your feelings: do you resent having too much to do or are you willing to put up with this for the sake of your career?

❑ One course of action is to negotiate your overload – to do this successfully you will have to plan your argument carefully and produce as much evidence as possible.

❑ Your second option is to say 'no' to any additional pieces of work. A refusal does not have to be heavy or hurtful; you can speak calmly and still acknowledge the other person's needs and feelings, even while you are saying 'no'.

❑ The third option is simply to change how you feel about the amount of work you have to do. The important point is to remember that it's not your fault that there is too much work to do – it has happened as a result of someone else's inefficiency or because of the organization's lack of resources.

The next chapter deals with a key time management technique – delegation.

5

DELEGATION

If you have too much work and too little time to do it, it makes sense to delegate some of it to other people. Many managers don't delegate as much work as they might to the people in their team. As a result, they get bogged down in routine operational tasks, rather than concentrating on the vital managerial functions of long-term planning, solving problems or developing new opportunities.

This chapter will help you to understand why delegation is a crucial part of your role as a manager. It will also give some guidance on identifying suitable tasks for delegation and on how to delegate effectively.

WHY DELEGATE?

Delegation is not easy: it requires courage, patience and careful planning. However, it is the single most important technique for generating time for yourself and securing a greater commitment from the people in your team. If you delegate properly, you will be able to trust others to carry out pieces of work which you would otherwise have to perform yourself.

When you delegate, you are giving someone else the responsibility to perform a task or a duty that is actually part of your own job. You are providing that person with the authority to make decisions and take the necessary action to complete the task. Although your team member is responsible to you for achieving the task, you are still responsible to higher management for getting the work done. You decide how the task should be performed and then instruct your team member accordingly.

Margo is Head of Staff Development at a university in the south of England. She was forced to delegate to her PA when she found that she was out of the office at least three days a week. The PA soon became so busy that she had to take on an assistant to do a lot of her own routine administrative work.

Delegating offers a number of advantages, for example:

❏ You will have more time to spend on items that are a central part of your role. A manager's job should be concerned with planning the future rather than organizing the present. If you are not thinking ahead, you will spend your time fire-fighting rather than planning how to stay ahead of the competition.

❏ People in your team will develop new skills and become more committed to achieving objectives and targets. Delegation does much for people's morale and job satisfaction. Good delegators experience less absenteeism and more willingness to work longer hours when the pressure is on.

In short, delegation lightens your workload, and develops your team's abilities at the same time. It is the best possible way of training people to take on new responsibilities.

MINIMIZING THE RISKS OF DELEGATION

There are many excuses for not delegating. Which of these have you used in the past?

❏ 'I don't have time to delegate.' ☐
❏ 'I can do the job better than anyone else.' ☐
❏ 'I enjoy this job. I've always done it.' ☐
❏ 'If I delegate too much, I'll be doing myself out of a job.' ☐

❏ 'I don't trust anyone to do such a good job as I can.' ☐

If you have used any of these reasons for not delegating, you need to change your attitude.

From:	To:
'I don't have time to delegate.'	'I have to make time – it will be a good investment in the long run.'
'I can do the job better than anyone else.'	'My job should not involve doing all the work myself – I have a responsibility to develop the people in my team.'
'I enjoy this job. I've always done it.'	'If I enjoy it, I will be able to explain it well and make others feel enthusiastic about it.'
'If I delegate too much, I'll be doing myself out of a job.'	'I'm already too busy to find time to attend to the important things.'
'I don't trust anyone to do such a good job as I can.'	'I have to accept that, although other people won't do things in exactly the same way, they will probably do them just as well.'

If you don't delegate, you may remain on the same old treadmill for ever. Remember that:

❏ it is an important part of your role to develop the skills of the people in your team;
❏ people will perform tasks better and quicker with guidance and practice;
❏ your skills could be better employed elsewhere.

There is no doubt that delegation is a risk because it involves reducing your direct control and relying on other people to perform effectively in order to get the job done. However, most problems that managers have with delegation can be eliminated with careful planning. To reduce the risks you can:

❑ select the tasks you delegate carefully;
❑ select the right people to do these tasks.

To delegate effectively, you have to accept that the process may be slow in the early stages and that there may well be setbacks. The problem for anyone who wants to manage their time is that at first you may become busier than ever. This is because, in addition to your normal workload, you will be supporting and coaching members of your team.

Suitable tasks for delegation

Before deciding on suitable tasks for delegation, you need to be clear about which ones are definitely unsuitable. In general terms, these are the tasks that are beyond the skills and experience of your team members – although you should be aware that most people can rise to a challenge if you give them the chance. Beware of delegating tasks which are so crucial that any extra risk of failure is unacceptable. As a normal rule, it would also be wrong to delegate tasks that relate to confidential or disciplinary matters.

Finally, you need to be cautious of delegating tasks which have been delegated to you. This is because you are responsible to the people who have reduced their direct control by delegating to you. You should only delegate this type of task once you have checked with the person concerned.

But after you have ruled out items that are too complex, too important or too confidential, there will still be a number of possibilities. These will include:

❑ routine tasks;
❑ tasks that require no special skills;
❑ tasks that are very time-consuming;

❑   tasks that have to be carried out at regular intervals;
❑   tasks that can be planned well in advance;
❑   tasks which someone else has a real interest in taking on.

> **Ross** is managing director of a small video production company. His policy is to delegate jobs that people will find interesting and stimulating, rather than ones that will bore them. He says that half the battle is won when people are enthusiastic about the tasks that they have been given.

Selecting the people

After confirming that a task is suitable for delegation, your next step is to decide whether any of your team members currently possess the skills required to perform the task. If not, could someone be trained or coached to do it?

Beware of trying to minimize the risks of failure by selecting someone who already has the skills to do the job. Although it may be more risky to select someone who is not the obvious choice, it may be worthwhile in the long term if the person can use the delegated task as a method of developing his or her skills.

Once you have identified a suitable person or people, ask yourself:

❑   would they enjoy doing this task?
❑   would their present workload allow them to take on the task? If not, is it possible to reallocate some of their existing workload?

Now plan how you will delegate one of your tasks.

What is the task?

Give two reasons why you think it is suitable for delegation:

✎

_____

_____

_____

✎

_____

_____

_____

Who could you delegate the task to?

✎

_____

_____

_____

Would he or she need any coaching to take on the task?

Yes ☐   No ☐

If 'yes', what coaching would you organize and who would do it?

✎

_____

_____

_____

How do you think the person would feel about you delegating this task to him or her?

HOW TO DELEGATE

Effective delegation involves working through four distinct steps.

1. Tell the team member what you are aiming to achieve.
2. Encourage him or her to take on ownership of the task.
3. Agree what information or support will be needed, and what deadlines to aim for.
4. Decide how you will monitor progress and evaluate the outcomes of the delegation.

Identifying objectives

It is important to identify what you want your team member to achieve. You should also reach a shared agreement about:

❑ the specific outcomes that you require, and
❑ the standard that you are expecting.

> When **Marie**, manager of a large touring theatre in Scotland, delegates work to her secretary, Ben, she always writes down the details of the job to be done. She finds that this practice makes her clarify what she wants. If Ben does not understand the task, it's often because Marie has not provided clear instructions.

Encouraging ownership of the task

Beware of being so specific that you leave your team member with no space for manoeuvre or personal initiative. When you delegate work, you state the objective – but the other person should have some freedom to decide on how the objective will be achieved.

If you don't allow people to carry out tasks in their own way, they will not be able to develop in a way that suits their own character and potential. People need to be free to decide how they will use the authority which has been delegated to them. They will sense very quickly how genuine your trust is by the way in which you delegate.

Imagine that you have asked a member of your team, Rosemary, to do a survey to find out the level of customer satisfaction with a particular product or service. A few weeks later she comes back and says that she is having some trouble with the job because only four out of 30 questionnaires have been returned. What do you do and say in these circumstances?

(a) 'Don't worry – I'm sending out a circular to all those customers this week. I shall pop in a reminder asking them to return the questionnaires as soon as possible.'

(b) 'Have you though of giving them a quick ring? People will often be happy to help after they have spoken to you in person. If you don't like that idea, perhaps you could send them a fax.'

For many of us response (a) is the obvious one, but the trouble with this is that you would be taking control away from Rosemary who, as a result, will no longer be doing the job you delegated. If you choose (a) you are trying to help but you will probably make her feel resentful or useless.

If you choose response (b), you are offering help and support, but you are leaving the choices and the authority with your team member. So the part of the job that you have delegated remains in Rosemary's hands and you will not have damaged her self-confidence. When you delegate, you must allow your team members to remain in charge of the task. It is unfair to give out authority with one hand and then snatch it back with the other at the first hint of a problem.

Information and support

It is vital to clarify what information, support and resources the person will need right from the beginning. In this way you can plan your own involvement into your schedule and you will not be in for any surprises.

Some people need a lot of support, while others just need to be told what the task is and they will get on with it. The latter type of person is a very valuable asset – make sure you don't abuse his or her ability by forgetting to ask how things are going or failing to show that you value the effort that is being made. Those people who need plenty of support may need to be weaned off their dependency – try building up their confidence with a bit of praise when the first part of the task is complete.

You can enlist the help of others in supporting the person to whom you are delegating. In fact, an important part of the process is for your 'delegate' to get used to asking a wide range of people for help and information. So don't try to be an expert on everything yourself. Get used to saying things like 'Joe's a good person to ask about that', or 'See how far Sue has got with her project – she may be able to give you the names of other people who can help.'

Monitoring progress

When you delegate work, you still have the responsibility for making sure that what you have planned to happen actually does happen. Monitoring enables you to ensure that you are meeting the responsibilities placed upon you by a higher authority – even though you are not carrying out the tasks personally. If you monitor regularly, you can spot problems early on and take appropriate action before they turn into real disasters.

Some managers may think that it is intrusive to keep a check on how people are getting on with the delegated task. If,

however, responsibilities and objectives have been openly nego-
tiated right from the beginning, this difficulty should not arise.

Here are some of the main techniques for monitoring progress:

❑ observing people while they work;
❑ examining the things that produce (letters, reports, or simply
an outcome);
❑ asking people how they are doing;
❑ chatting informally over a cup of coffee;
❑ collecting and analysing statistical data;
❑ obtaining feedback from other team members or customers.

The most important point is to make time to walk about, to
show that you care about your staff and about how they are
getting on. It should take only a few minutes a day (any more
and you may be actually keeping them from their work), but it
allows you to detect problems before they become serious.

If you spot something that looks as if it's going wrong, it is
best not make it a major issue. For reasons we have already
discussed, you must avoid the temptation to jump in and take
control. Instead, have a quiet word to make sure that the person
concerned is aware of what's happening and knows how to put
things right. It is important to make it clear that you trust him
or her to handle the situation, but that you are always there to
help if necessary.

Evaluating the outcomes of the delegation

Whereas monitoring takes place while a task is being carried
out, evaluation occurs when it has been completed. It means
standing back and deciding how well the task has been achieved
and what should happen next. Evaluation has a vital role to
play in improving your effectiveness as a delegator because it
will provide you with important information that will enable
you to do better next time.

Because you are still accountable for the tasks you delegate,
you need to find out whether the objectives have been met.
Depending on the nature of the task, you may need to answer
questions like:

❏ Were all the objectives met?
❏ Has the task been completed within the budget?
❏ Did I provide enough of the right kind of information and support?
❏ Was the task completed on time?
❏ How effective was the monitoring?
❏ Did we deal with problems in the right way?
❏ Was it completed to the standard I was expecting?

If the answer to any of these questions is 'no', then you need to find out why so that you and others can learn from any mistakes made.

If there are shortfalls in performance you will need to ask questions like:

❏ Was the original task properly specified, or was further unforeseen work required?
❏ Was the team member sidetracked with other work?
❏ Did the team member have the necessary skills?
❏ Were the budget, timescales and my expectations realistic?

Once you have analysed what, if anything, went wrong you can then decide how the planning stage could be improved the next time you delegate.

Now plan how you will delegate the task that you identified earlier in the chapter.

1. What are the objectives of this task?

✎

_____

_____

_____

_____

2. How will you encourage the person concerned to take on ownership of the task?

✎

_____

_____

_____

3. What information will he or she need?

✎

_____

_____

_____

4. What kind of support will he or she need?

✎

_____

_____

_____

5. What deadline will you set for the task?

✎

_____

_____

_____

6. How will you monitor progress?

✎

_____

_____

7. What questions will you need to ask when you are evaluating
the task?

GIVING FEEDBACK

Giving effective feedback is an essential part of the delegation
process – not just when you have completed an evaluation of
the final outcome, but also as a continuous process while the
work is being carried out. It is a major factor in the motivation
of your team and an important way of making sure that they
get things right.

Feedback makes people more aware of their strengths and
weaknesses. It helps them to:

❑ improve their performance the next time they carry out a
   task;
❑ build on their acknowledged successes;
❑ take a new perspective on their problems and concerns;
❑ know that what they do is appreciated.

Feedback is not just a matter of letting people know when
something has gone wrong so that they can avoid repeating the
mistake. It is equally important that you notice when things
have gone well so that you reinforce effective work practices.
Effective feedback is empowering because it contributes to
people's self-awareness. If it is competently given, it should also

leave recipients with a choice – they do not have to act on the feedback unless they wish to do so.

The trouble is that feedback is often confused with criticism, and it is somehow much easier to criticize than to give feedback. The table below summarizes some of the differences between feedback and criticism.

Criticism:	Feedback:
❏ Focuses on the person	❏ Focuses on issues or problems
❏ Harks back to the past	❏ Looks to the future
❏ Allocates blame	❏ Looks for joint solutions to problems
❏ Makes generalizations	❏ Deals with particular episodes or situations
❏ Says 'always' or 'never'	❏ Makes specific comments
❏ Starts from a position of hostility or aggression	❏ Always uses a positive, friendly approach

Constructive feedback

To avoid criticizing, it is valuable to develop the skills of giving constructive feedback, which is a combination of positive and negative feedback. Constructive feedback does not make value judgements or personal comments. As you are offering a personal view, the recipient can choose whether or not to agree with your opinion.

Your comments on work that you have delegated should have the following qualities:

1. *Honest*. Your have to say what you really think. Your people may misunderstand the points you are making if you try to soften them so that your comments are muddled. If you have

a genuine desire to help what you have to say will be taken in the right spirit.

2. *Objective.* At all costs you have to avoid a 'knee-jerk' or 'gut' reaction, which may be value-laden or emotionally charged. If the feedback is really important it is best to write down what you want to say or practise first with someone else. If there is no time to practise before giving the feedback, at least try to take a few breaths and gather your thoughts for a moment before speaking.

3. *Positive.* If they are to improve, people need to know where their strengths are as well as where you think they need to put in some effort. Furthermore, if you prove that you recognize and value their positive points, people are more likely to act on the negative ones.

4. *Specific.* It does not matter whether you are offering positive or negative feedback, both should be specific statements relating to a person's work or behaviour. Statements such as, 'Not good enough' or 'an excellent job' do not give enough useful information to allow someone to learn. It is much more valuable to identify exactly what the person did that was not good or excellent.

5. *Timely.* You need to tell staff that things are going wrong as soon as you can. Don't leave it until a task has been poorly completed. By monitoring, you are able to prevent your staff from wasting time and effort while they are carrying out their tasks.

Finally, if you want people to listen to you and to take responsibility for the results they achieve you must:

❑ *Own the feedback* – it can be extremely daunting for recipients of feedback if you give them to understand that you are providing universally held views about them. If, on the other hand, you say something like, 'I believe', or 'in my view', however, it helps to convey the impression that what you are saying is your opinion.

❑ *Leave the recipient with a choice* – you may encounter resistance if your feedback demands that a person behave in a certain way. If he or she does what you suggest, this may only be because you are piling on the pressure. To encourage people to take responsibility you must give feedback in such a way that recipients feel that they can decide whether to act on it or not. If what they do is their decision, they will take more responsibility for their own actions and the consequences of these.

Next time you delegate, give some constructive feedback and use the above guidelines to make sure that what you say has the effect of encouraging the person concerned to continue to do a good job.

SUMMARY

The aim of this chapter has been to help you to use delegation to make more time for important tasks.

❑ When you delegate, you are giving someone else the responsibility to perform a task or a duty that is actually part of your own job. At the same time you are providing that person with the authority to make decisions and take the necessary action to complete the task.

❑ The problem for those people who want to manage their time is that at first you may become busier than ever because you will be supporting and coaching members of your team, in addition to your normal workload.

❑ You should delegate tasks that are straightforward, routine or repetitive. Don't delegate ones that are too complex, too important or too confidential.

❑ Choose the people on the basis of their skills or their potential or because they would find the task challenging or enjoyable.

❑ Effective delegation involves working through four distinct steps:
— telling the team member what you are aiming to achieve;
— encouraging him or her to take on ownership of the task;

Continued on next page

— agreeing what information or support will be needed, and what deadlines to aim for;

— deciding how you will monitor progress and evaluate the outcomes of the delegation.

❑ Giving feedback is an essential part of the delegation process. It is a major way of motivating your team and making sure they get things right.

❑ Make sure that your feedback is:

— honest;

— objective;

— positive;

— specific;

— timely;

and that you:

— own the feedback; and

— leave the recipient with a choice

The next chapter looks at some other techniques for effective time management.

6

SOME TECHNIQUES FOR TIME MANAGEMENT

This final chapter will focus on some of the most effective techniques for making better use of the time you have available. At the end you are invited to choose the solutions that best suit your own problems and plan how to integrate these approaches into your work and your life.

We shall look at ways of:

❑ making meetings more effective;
❑ tackling paperwork efficiently;
❑ producing reader-friendly paperwork;
❑ reading more effectively;
❑ avoiding procrastination;
❑ controlling interruptions;
❑ using the telephone more efficiently.

MAKING MEETINGS MORE EFFECTIVE

Meetings are one of the top time wasters in business organizations – yet they are a vital tool for keeping people informed and for making things happen. One problem with meetings is that, unless you are very careful, they can go on too long, they can wander off the point and they can leave people feeling irritated and discontented.

George is a local government officer. When he first joined his section, he used to feel irritated because he believed that a lot of time was wasted during his weekly team meetings. In the end he took the initiative and suggested that the team set start and finish times for the meetings and that each item on the agenda should be allocated a time slot.

Do your meetings:

❏ start and finish on time? □
❏ have a clear purpose and objectives? □
❏ keep to the point? □
❏ enable all participants to contribute in some way? □
❏ include topics that are relevant for everyone who □
   attends?
❏ leave people satisfied that the time spent in the meeting □
   was well spent?

If you ticked less than three of the above, you should consider ways of making your meetings shorter and more effective.

Below we have listed six key criteria for transforming meetings from dull, time-wasting gatherings into enjoyable and empowering experiences.

1. *They should be planned and prepared well in advance*. If the agenda and any (brief) accompanying papers are drawn up and circulated at least a week before the meetings take place, participants will have time to familiarize themselves with the contents of these items. This will save time and will make the meeting more effective.

   Part of your planning should involve setting a start and finish time for the meeting and making sure that it is as short as possible. People become very tired and distracted in events that go on for three hours or more. If you have to run a long meeting, make sure that you plan frequent breaks, so that participants have the opportunity to stretch their limbs and get some fresh air.

---

2. *Everyone should be aware of the purpose or objectives of the meeting.* Again this simple point is all too often omitted from business meetings. Yet it is amazing how much more effective they can be when everyone is aware of the expected outcome. If the point is not clarified by the start of the meeting, it should become the first agenda item.

   Part of the role of the chairperson is to keep drawing the focus of the discussion back to the agreed objectives. This will make sure that people don't waste time by wandering off the point.

3. *The time available should be appropriately structured.* Again, if this has not been decided beforehand, you should start the proceedings by allotting a certain amount of time to each agenda item. This will help everyone to agree and clarify the relative priorities of the different points. The chairperson then should encourage everyone to be brief so that the time deadlines are achieved.

4. *Participants should be encouraged to communicate effectively.* It is often left to the person chairing the meeting to ask for clarification, to summarize or to check for understanding or agreement. But if all participants see it as part of their responsibility to do these things for the group, the discussion will be more focused, less time will be wasted and fewer misunderstandings will occur.

5. *The meeting should be effectively facilitated.* A good 'chair' or facilitator can sometimes make the difference between an excellent meeting and a poor one. Such a person can keep everyone on track, eliminate repetition and ensure that everyone present has the opportunity to make a contribution.

   If you don't have an effective facilitator or chairperson, it may be worth selecting a suitable person and providing him or her with the right sort of training. Another approach would be to ask someone with appropriate skills from outside the group to take on this role.

6. *Participants should review the effectiveness of the meeting.* It is useful to spend some time at the end of a meeting reviewing how it went. If participants are honest, they can provide feedback and ideas that will improve things the next time.

To do this properly it would be useful to agree some 'success indicators' against which participants can review their performance.

For example, people may agree that the meeting will have been successful if it:
— starts and finishes on time;
— gives everyone a chance to contribute;
— achieves its objectives;
— and so on.

If some of these criteria are not met, part of the review could focus on how to remedy things the next time.

Clarifying the purpose

Meetings that make the best use of the time available don't just happen, they have to be worked at. One of the best ways of improving the effectiveness of the meetings you organize or take part in is to clarify the reason for holding the meeting. If a meeting has no real purpose, it should not take place at all. That may seem obvious, but it is surprising how many gatherings happen just of habit, or because people do not feel confident enough to make a decision without calling everyone in.

Before you can begin a meeting, you and the other participants need to clarify exactly what you want it to achieve. Meetings bring together the expertise and experience of a certain group of people. The aim may be to give information to them or to seek information from them. The purpose of the meeting may be to make a decision, solve a problem, resolve a conflict or simply to review the progress of a project and to move it on to the next phase. Good meetings also serve to bring a group closer together by promoting interaction among team members.

Colin is a transport manager with an oil company. When he plans a meeting, he always writes out what he perceives as its main aim and makes sure everyone knows what this is. If he is attending a meeting
Continued on next page

that seems to have no real focus, he tries to work out what he thinks its purpose might be and then checks that everyone's idea is the same as his. At least he knows then that the meeting is less likely to waste everyone's time by wandering off the point.

TACKLING PAPERWORK EFFICIENTLY

Many of us feel overwhelmed by the amount of paper we receive; there are simply not enough hours in the working day to read everything we are presented with. But if we don't make time to deal with it, we run the risk of being swamped by a tidal wave of reports, journals, memos, letters, books, brochures and all kinds of other documents.

Often the result is that much of it doesn't get tackled at all, and there's a niggling feeling that there might be something important in that large pile that is teetering on the far right-hand corner of the desk. If you don't have a system for coping with paperwork, it could mean all sorts of problems – lost business, irritated customers, ignorance of vital information, lack of familiarity with new ideas and so on. You won't just feel disorganised and hopeless, you will miss out on the things you need to know and your performance will suffer as a result.

The one touch approach

The 'one touch approach' is a way of sorting out which papers you need to deal with immediately, which ones you should spend more time on and which you can safely ignore or throw away. As its name suggests, this approach disciplines you to handling each piece of paper once only. If you are not sure that this approach is right for you, try putting a dot on a document every time you handle it. If there is a polka dot effect, you'll find it useful to take a more decisive approach in dealing with each item immediately.

Martia is an A&R manager in a record company. She often writes a note on the incoming letter or memo rather than taking time to write a more formal reply.

Much of the paperwork we receive is of little or no relevance to our goals and needs. So an effective first step towards the control of paperwork is to sort it into categories. Each category would require a different type of action. For example:

❏ *papers that relate to your key goals or priorities*: mark these clearly and set aside time for reading them;
❏ *papers that relate to non-priority work*: mark them for filing in the appropriate place so that you will be able to find and read them when you have time;
❏ *papers that relate to urgent work*: deal with these immediately, but don't spend too much time on them;
❏ *items you can delegate*: pass these on to the person concerned immediately;
❏ *items that have no relevance to any of your goals*: pass them on immediately to the people to whom they are relevant or put them straight into the waste paper basket.

It is often difficult to determine how useful written material will be until you have actually looked through it. Use the checklist below to scan your 'priority reading' pile and to decide whether each item will be as useful as it may at first seem:

❏ look at the title;
❏ look at the summary/introductory paragraph;
❏ look at the conclusions/recommendations;
❏ skim through the main headings.

PRODUCING READER-FRIENDLY PAPERWORK

You will help others to avoid wasting time if you produce paperwork that is easy to read and understand. There are two benefits from producing reader-friendly paperwork:

❑   it will save you time;
❑   it will minimize the amount of paper you load onto other people.

Next time you need to write a letter, memo or report use this checklist to help you to plan and prepare it.

❑   Get organized – collect all the relevant information and papers before you start.
❑   Consider whether a written document is appropriate – would a telephone call be quicker and cheaper?
❑   Prepare an outline of the key points you need to raise – a few notes for a letter, a list of section headings for a report.
❑   Structure the document to include introduction, main points and conclusions. For reports, consider a summary of the main points at the end.
❑   Consider using a dictating machine to save time – but beware of becoming verbose.
❑   KISS – Keep It Simple and Short. Use simple language and limit yourself to necessary information and words.
❑   Use standard letters and paragraphs for repetitive work.
❑   Avoid over-editing. This can become a temptation with word processing and can consume a lot of time.

Writing for readability

It doesn't matter whether your readers are highly paid executives, academics involved in research or a team of maintenance engineers working on the shop floor – everyone needs to receive material that they find easy to read and assimilate.

Unfortunately, it is not unusual for people who communicate clearly when they are speaking to express themselves in a complicated and clumsy way when they sit down to write. Many of us have been taught at school to write in a rather impersonal, indirect way and to believe that long words and sentences are more appropriate than short ones on the page. However, the closer you can get to a writing style which sounds as though you are talking directly to the reader, the more readable your writing will be.

❏ *Sentences*. You will make a piece of writing more digestible if you use a number of short sentences rather than fewer long sentences. Try to ensure that there is only one main idea in each sentence.

❏ *Paragraphs*. Paragraphs should not be too long, ideally about five to ten lines. Each paragraph should contain a number of sentences which are clearly linked to a single topic.

❏ *Vocabulary*. Use simple and familiar words wherever possible. This does not mean patronizing the reader by using words of one syllable, but using the most common and straightforward language to express what you want to say.

Here are some words and phrases that are often found in business documents, try translating them into more everyday language.

In the vicinity of

Prior to

At this point in time

Procure

In spite of the fact that

✎

In order to

✎

Has a tendency to

✎

Elevate

✎

Due to the fact that

✎

A high proportion of

✎

Remember that writing for readability does not mean that you can never use long words or sentences, rather that you should restrict these to occasions when they are absolutely necessary.

READING FASTER AND MORE EFFICIENTLY

Reading more effectively is rapidly becoming a vital skill for busy people who are faced with mountains of reading material. Yet the average reading speed is only 240 words per minute – and many people can recall only a small proportion of what they have read a day later.

This quick test will help you to decide if you could improve your reading speed.

Do you:

❏ believe that you are already reading as fast as you can? ☐
❏ lose concentration very easily? ☐
❏ allow your eyes to wander off the page? ☐
❏ read only one word at a time? ☐
❏ allow your eyes to back skip – to check what you have ☐
just read?

If you ticked more than two of the above, your reading speed may well be below 200 words per minute. This in turn means that you are making it harder for yourself to understand and retain much of what you read, and you are not making maximum use of the reading time available.

If you want to check your current reading speed, time yourself as you read a passage from any book or document. Set your watch or a timer for one minute and see how many words you can read in that time. The following table will give you some basic signposts to reading performance.

Words per minute	Standard achieved
10–100	Poor
200–240	Average
400	Good
800–1000	Top 1%
1000 +	Top 0.01%

Don't worry if you got a low score this time. You can increase your speed quite easily if you practise the techniques described below.

Speeding up

You will read faster and more efficiently if you take time to preview the text before you study it in more detail. As you skim and scan through the headings, the beginnings and ends of paragraphs and any pictures or charts, you will get a good idea of its purpose and intended readership. If the document is not valuable or borrowed, you will find it useful to make notes in the margin or to highlight those parts that you feel will be worth special attention later. This preview will provide you with a skeleton outline of the text – you are then ready to put meat on the bones with a more thorough, but fast, reading of the whole thing.

Here are four techniques for reading faster:

1. *Eliminate back skipping*. People back skip because they lack confidence in their ability to understand what they read in one go. You should be able to take in at least 90 per cent of the information the first time you read it. If it is important to understand the other 10 per cent, you can always read the whole document a second time.

2. *Take in groups of words rather than single words*. When we read a sentence we do not read it for the individual meaning of each word, but for the meaning of the phrases in which the words are contained. You can therefore make comprehension easier by expanding the number of words you fix on. With practice you can take in as many as three to five words at a time.

3. *Don't allow your eyes to wander off the line or the page*. If you discipline yourself to keep focusing on the line of text, you are less likely to be distracted and lose concentration.

4. *Use a pointer*. This helps your eye to speed up and will help you to establish a smooth rhythmical habit. You are not restricted to the use of your forefinger as a visual aid. You can use a pen or a pencil, or even a knitting needle. Place your pointer at an angle of 45 degrees under the first word at the left-hand side of the first line of text. Smoothly sweep the pointer along the line until you get to the end, then lift the pointer and place it under the first word on the next line.

Taking in more than one line at a time is not physically imposs-ible and is especially useful when you are scanning through light material or previewing something that you intend to study in more detail at a later date. It is very important to use a visual guide during this kind of reading, as without it the eye will tend to wander with comparatively little direction over the page.

Once you have mastered these techniques, measure your reading speed again – it is certain that it will be faster this time. Many people find that using a pointer feels strange at first, but you will get used to it with practice. Others say that using these techniques makes them lose comprehension. This is not surprising because at first you will be concentrating harder on the techniques than on what you are supposed to be reading. In time you will read faster and your comprehension will improve too.

REDUCING PROCRASTINATION

Planning how to use your time will inevitably involve putting some things off till a later date. The trick is to make active decisions about what you do now and what you do later. Just letting things slide will just leave you feeling anxious and out of control.

To reduce procrastination you have to identify the types of job you put off, and explore the excuses you make and the reasons why you do so. Finding the reasons really means finding out about yourself – your attitudes, and your fears – so that you can identify techniques for overcoming these blocks to productive work.

Sally is a managing director's PA. Because she is under so much pressure, she often puts off really big jobs till the last possible moment to meet the deadline. She used to say that she works best under pressure but she now thinks that she would produce much better results if she gave herself more time.

In fact, people often say that they work best under pressure, and this strategy does actually seem to work for some people. However, have you ever considered that if you always leave things till the last minute:

❑ you eventually become less efficient;
❑ you may feel guilty or angry with yourself;
❑ everything else will go by the board as the deadline approaches;
❑ you may waste time and energy worrying about the task you have put off;
❑ your health, your family and other parts of your life may eventually suffer.

Excuses and reasons

Most people don't realize how much they procrastinate until they sit down to analyse real situations.

1. Which types of jobs do you put off?

✎

_____

_____

_____

_____

2. Why do you put them off?

✎

_____

_____

_____

_____

3. What are the consequences of putting these jobs off?

✎ _____

_____

_____

_____

Here are some of the many excuses and reasons that people give for procrastinating. Which ones do you identify with?

❑ Some things seem really unpleasant or daunting so I can't face doing them.

❑ I catch myself saying that I don't have time to do something – when really I just don't want to do it.

❑ I often think that if I put something off for long enough, someone else will do it eventually.

❑ I procrastinate when I believe that I won't be able to do a particular job.

❑ Sometimes I just don't know where or how to begin – so I delay making a start till the last minute.

❑ I often put something off if I'm anxious that there won't be time to do the job well.

❑ I'll do anything rather than tackle writing a report which I hate. I can fiddle around for hours doing the easy or unimportant jobs instead – like bringing the client database up to date, ordering stationery or watering the plants.

If you procrastinate a lot, you may feel guilty, anxious, bored or a combination of all three. You may experience a number of problems, including decisions not made, missed opportunities or failure to complete tasks. If you are not being honest with yourself, your confidence and self-esteem will suffer and this factor will act as a barrier to your personal development.

Attitudes and techniques

Overcoming procrastination is largely a matter of changing how you feel about certain types of job. Can you:

❏ Face up to the fact that you have been wasting time in the past? If you admit that you procrastinate, you can start to do something about the problem.

❏ Take a more positive attitude to work? You could start to look at the benefits of doing the work – not just the things you hate.

❏ Recognize that you get no satisfaction at all from doing the easy jobs? On the other hand, you will get a real boost from completing the tasks that you find challenging or unpleasant.

❏ Accept that a job is not going to go away if you procrastinate? It will only get worse if you put it off . . .

❏ Make up your mind to face up to unpleasant tasks?

❏ Think about previous jobs that you have completed and recognize that you have rarely (if ever) failed in the past?

People use a number of techniques for overcoming procrastination. One of these may work for you.

❏ Plan how you will tackle a daunting job the evening before you intend to start. Then carry out your plan without stopping to think.

❏ Do the worst job first.

❏ Break a big job down into small tasks.

❏ If getting started is the main problem, don't start at the beginning, start anywhere. The important thing is to make a start!

❏ Commit yourself by telling someone that you are going to do the job.

❏ If you haven't got a deadline – set your own.

❏ Reward yourself at stages throughout the job and when it is finished.

❏ Avoid the things that distract you (socializing etc.).

❏ Set time aside in your diary for doing a job you hate.

❏ Don't allow yourself to stop until you have worked for at least one hour.

This list of techniques is not exhaustive – if you set your mind to it you will be able to think of other ways of reducing procrastination. Ask your friends and colleagues how they tackle the problem and add their ideas to your own list. Most people find that procrastination is actually just a habit. It can be overcome by learning new habits and telling yourself that you *can* change if you want to do so.

Huw is a supermarket manager. He doesn't mind giving out praise but always puts off having to inform people that their work is not up to scratch. He has to tell himself that it's an important part of his job and that if he fails to carry it out, he's not helping the store or the person concerned. He tries to be as objective and positive as possible, and it's never as bad as he thinks it's going to be.

CONTROLLING INTERRUPTIONS

If you have kept a time log as we suggest in the first chapter of this book, you may have found that an enormous amount of time is taken up with interruptions. Your best laid plans for the day – and ultimately for your entire life – may be thrown into disarray if you allow interruptions to distract you from what you have planned to do. By finding out more about your interruptions, you can take steps to reduce both their number and the amount of time they take up.

What causes your interruptions?

If you have completed a time log, you may already be aware of the kinds of things that can bring your work to a temporary halt. If not, you may like to keep a record of your interruptions for a whole week, recording:

❏ who or what caused the interruption;
❏ the method of interruption (visit/phone);
❏ how much time was taken up in each case.

Once you have this information, try to make some sense of it by answering the following questions:

1. How much time did you spend dealing with interruptions during that week?

✎
_____

_____

_____

2. What proportion of the interruptions were important or unavoidable?

✎
_____

_____

_____

3. What are the main causes of your interruptions?

✎
_____

_____

_____

4. When do the interruptions take place?

✎
_____

_____

_____

5. Do you interrupt yourself? If so, how?

✎

When you have done this analysis you will probably start to see a pattern or a problem emerging. It may be that several hours are taken up in a typical week with unnecessary interruptions. You may have been able to identify the main causes of these interruptions – for example constant crises, other people wanting to have a chat, your boss asking you to do something. The interruptions may take place at a particular time – first thing in the morning, for example, or on Wednesdays when the boss is out visiting customers. And you may or may not be surprised to learn that one of the main causes of your interruptions is yourself – by stopping to make a phone call, to have a cup of tea or a chat with colleagues.

Techniques

Once you have worked out who or what is causing the interruptions, you can then decide on a strategy for controlling them.

Leonie is a human resources manager in a water company. She says that one of the main drawbacks of working in an open plan office is that colleagues often pop over to her desk for a chat. She admits that nine out ten times it's about work – but it's usually something that relates to their priorities, not hers. Leonie tried to discourage such interruptions, but she has not found it easy because people thought she was being unfriendly. In the end she brought it up as subject for discussion at the monthly team meeting, and she was surprised to discover that this was a problem for others too.

In the end the team agreed to reinstate the coffee break, and to use this time to discuss urgent matters or make appointments with each other for informal meetings at mutually convenient times. Leonie doesn't think the problem will go away immediately, but at least the others now understand that she is not being rude if she doesn't want to be interrupted when she is trying to concentrate.

This checklist can help you to work out your own strategies for reducing the number of interruptions, for controlling the interruptions when they take place and for reducing your own interruptions. If the sheer number of interruptions is a problem, can you:

❑ cut down on the number of phone interruptions by routing phone calls through your assistant or secretary? He or she could then deal with routine matters.
❑ use an answerphone to 'screen' phone calls – and only take the urgent ones? Then deal with the low priority calls in batches when you have time.
❑ ask colleagues to take messages for you when you are working on an important task? Do the same for them when they need some time undisturbed.
❑ receive visitors 'by appointment only'?
❑ make it clear that you are not available for socializing during working hours? If people pop in for a chat you could say you will see them at coffee break or at lunch time.
❑ close your door or put up a 'do not disturb' notice?
❑ tell some visitors firmly but politely that you are busy and cannot be interrupted?

Clare is production manager in a garment factory. Her first task of the day is to deal with any urgent messages that have come in overnight. Her second is to take a walk around the office and the workrooms – the aim being to make herself available to anyone who wants to have a chat or arrange to see her privately. She also uses that time to give the staff any important information and to check that all the equipment is in good working order. Then she goes back to her office with the aim of working undisturbed for about two hours. After that her door is open for a while so that people can pop in. In the afternoon she has another quiet session. Everyone now knows that if the door is closed she can't be interrupted unless it is extremely urgent.

If the length of interruptions is a problem, can you:

❏ set a limit on the amount of time you can spare for a meeting or phone call and stick to it?
❏ cut down on the social talk and politely ask the person to get to the point?
❏ avoid asking unexpected visitors to sit down and remain standing yourself?
❏ set an egg timer for incoming phone calls?
❏ arrange to meet in another person's office, so that you can end the meeting more easily?
❏ practise bringing conversations to an end in a polite but firm manner?

If interrupting yourself is a problem, can you:

❏ refuse to allow yourself to become distracted?
❏ reward yourself if you can work for a certain amount of time without becoming distracted?
❏ give yourself regular breaks at pre-set times?
❏ organize your office or working environment in a way that will minimize distractions?
❏ arrange to meet friends and colleagues for coffee or lunch if you enjoy socializing?

As well as trying to reduce the number and the length of other people's interruptions, you should, of course, be making sure that you are not interrupting other people. Try to be a role model for good practice yourself and you'll be surprised how many people will follow what you do.

YOUR ACTION PLAN

Use the action plan below to note down any actions – however modest – that you are going to take to improve the way you manage your time.

Activity	What you will do	When
Goal-setting and planning how to achieve these Making better use of planning tools (diaries, planners, schedules)		
Listing, prioritizing and allocating time to tasks		
Negotiating my overload		
Saying 'no' to more work		
Delegating effectively		
Making meetings more effective		
Tackling paperwork efficiently		
Producing reader-friendly paperwork		
Reading faster and more efficiently		
Reducing procrastination		
Controlling interruptions		

SUMMARY

The aim of this chapter has been to examine some simple techniques that you can use to make the best use of your time.

❑ You looked at six key criteria for transforming meetings from dull, time-wasting gatherings into enjoyable and empowering experiences.

❑ You examined the 'one touch approach' – a way of sorting out which papers you need to deal with immediately, which ones you should spend more time on and which you can safely ignore or throw away.

❑ You studied some guidelines for producing paperwork that is brief and easy to understand. You should use simple and familiar words and your sentences and paragraphs should be short.

❑ You learned how to improve your reading speed by eliminating back skipping, keeping your eyes on the page and using a pointer.

❑ You looked at some tips for reducing procrastination. To do this you first have to identify the types of job you put off, and explore the excuses you make and the reasons why you do so.

❑ You saw that, by finding out more about your interruptions, you can take steps to reduce both their number and the amount of time they take up.

Ultimately, managing our time better means reassessing our priorities and taking responsibility for what we do with our lives. Those of us who spend our days hurrying and chasing and making ourselves ill have forgotten one important thing. We do have plenty of time. But what we have to do is take it away from the things that don't matter.

INDEX